Bürgin Nissen Wentzlaff
Architekten
Bürgin Nissen Wentzlaff
Architects

Bürgin Nissen Wentzlaff Architekten
Zwei Seiten
Bürgin Nissen Wentzlaff Architects
Two Sides

Birkhäuser Verlag
Basel · Boston · Berlin

Einleitung
Introduction

Projekte brauchen für die Realisierung eine lange Zeit. Parallel zu diesem langsamen Rhythmus entwickeln sich die Ideen im Kopf des Architekten nach einem anderen zeitlichen Massstab. Besonders wenn er sein Bezugsnetz auch ausserhalb des eigenen Berufsfeldes sucht, können tagtägliche Knochenarbeit und Eindrücke von Büchern oder Reisen nur selten zur Deckung kommen.

Hinzu kommt, dass im Büro Bürgin Nissen Wentzlaff Architekten drei Partner aus verschiedenen Generationen, mit verschiedenen Ausbildungen tätig sind. Die langjährige Zusammenarbeit von Edi Bürgin mit Timothy Nissen und später mit Daniel Wentzlaff in eine einheitliche Form zu pressen wäre nur durch Zensur, Unterdrückung oder rückwirkende Vereinheitlichung möglich.

Im vorliegenden Buch wird die zeitlich versetzte Zweigleisigkeit im Denken der Architekten bewusst thematisiert: Während auf den rechten Seiten Bauten und Projekte der letzten 15 Jahre chronologisch dargestellt werden, dokumentiert die linke Seite die persönlichen Interessen und theoretischen Arbeiten der Architekten. Jede Seite läuft nach eigenen Gesetzen chronologisch ab. Reibungen und Widersprüchlichkeiten zwischen den «zwei Seiten» werden nicht unterdrückt, sondern – im Gegenteil – als Qualitätsmerkmal des Berufes bewusst aktiviert.

It takes a long time for a project to come to fruition. It is a slow-paced process. Running parallel to this process, but following a different rhythm, are the ideas developing in the architect's mind. Especially when the architect's frames of reference extend well beyond his immediate professional sphere, his workaday labours will rarely function in tandem with the impressions he has gleaned from books or travel.

The effects of such "asynchronism" are compounded when architects as unlike as the three partners of the practice Bürgin Nissen Wentzlaff Architekten collaborate – men of different generations and different training. Nothing short of censorship, suppression or retrospective standardization would be able to press the long-ongoing collaboration between Edi Bürgin, Timothy Nissen and later Daniel Wentzlaff into the same mould.

The present book consciously addresses this twin-track approach that occurs on a shifted time-scale in architects' thinking: the right-hand pages present buildings and projects over the last 15 years chronologically, while the left-hand pages record the architects' personal interests and theoretical work. Each page runs chronologically according to its own rules. Friction and contradictions between the "two sides" are not suppressed; on the contrary, they are purposely encouraged as a distinctive mark of the profession.

Inhalt
Contents

Beiträge
Contributions

Projekte
Projects

Nach-Fragen
Inquiries

von Carl Fingerhuth
Carl Fingerhuth **CF** befragt Edi Bürgin **EB**, Timothy O. Nissen **TON**, Daniel Wentzlaff **DW**
by Carl Fingerhuth
Carl Fingerhuth CF interviews Edi Bürgin EB, Timothy O. Nissen TON, Daniel Wentzlaff DW

Zusammen-Arbeit

CF Mich fasziniert bei Euren Arbeiten das breite Spektrum Eurer Tätigkeiten. Angefangen bei der Stadtplanung, dort habe ich Timmy Nissen in einer nach aussen orientierten, beinahe politischen Rolle kennengelernt. In meiner Funktion als Bauherr habe ich später Edi Bürgin als eher nach innen gekehrten Architekten erfahren und schliesslich Daniel Wentzlaff durch kreative Beiträge aus der Welt seiner Bilder, durch seine Arbeiten als Künstler.

Meiner Meinung nach wird das immer wichtiger: Dass wir Architekten Verständnis entwickeln für Zusammenhänge zwischen den Veränderungen der Stadt bis hin zur Qualität und Gestalt des einzelnen Objekts. Was bedeutet das in Eurer Arbeit?

TON Wir sehen diese Vielfalt als Bereicherung an. Ich bin ursprünglich in einer Schule der Deckungsgleichheit erzogen worden: Das heisst, dass man sich angemessen benehmen, die «Überstände» abschleifen und nach aussen ein einheitliches Bild abgeben muss. Erst kürzlich ist mir anhand der Ausstellung von Daniel wieder aufgefallen, dass man unsere Charaktere nie völlig zur Deckung bringen kann. Die Qualität unserer Zusammenarbeit liegt in den verschiedenen Interessensbildern.

DW Wir funktionieren wie Teilmengen mit einer gemeinsamen Schnittmenge. Dadurch ist der Gesamterfahrungsschatz, über den das Büro verfügt, breiter gefächert.

TON Auch technische Ökonomie und administrative Leistungen sind für ein gutes Büro erforderlich.
Zudem sind die Schnitt- und Teilmengen eine Herausforderung: Wenn der das kann, sollte ich es

Co-Operation

CF What fascinates me about your work is the wide spectrum of your activities. Let's start with town planning. I met Timmy Nissen in that context in an outward-looking, almost political role. Then, in my function as client, I came across Edi Bürgin a rather more inward-looking architect, and finally Daniel Wentzlaff through his work as an artist and the creative output from his world of pictures. In my opinion it is becoming increasingly important that we architects should develop an understanding of links between changes in cities and the quality and design of individual objects. What does that mean for your work?

TON We see this diversity as an enrichment. I was brought up in a "school of conformity": this means that one was told to behave appropriately, smooth down any "rough edges" and make things look uniform from the outside. It struck me only recently at Daniel's exhibition that our three characters can never be made to fit together completely. The quality of our co-operation lies in our various patterns of interest.

DW We function like subsets with a common area of intersection. This means that the overall pool of experience at the office's disposal is more wide-ranging.

TON Technical economy and administrative skills are also needed for a good office. At the same time the intersection area and the subsets are a challenge: if he can do that I should be able to do it too, or at least to understand it.

CF Can you explain that with an example of your work?

Umbau und Erweiterung einer Bankfiliale am Claraplatz, Basel, UBS Schweizerische Bankgesellschaft, 1983-1987
Conversion and Extension of a Bank Branch on Claraplatz, Basel, UBS Schweizerische Bankgesellschaft, 1983-1987

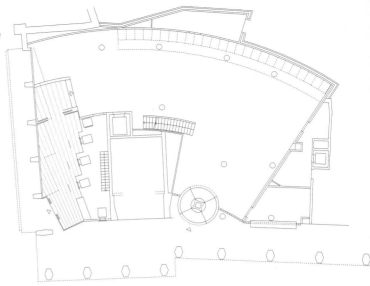

Die UBS wollte am Claraplatz in Basel ihre Präsenz wesentlich verbessern und ihr Angebot an bedienten Schaltern und Automaten vergrössern.

Mit einem Kreisbogen wird die bestehende, zweigeteilte Grundfläche zu einem einheitlichen Raumerlebnis verbunden. Unterstützt wird diese Geste durch ein der runden Wand folgendes Oberlicht und durch ein Neonlichtobjekt des Künstlers Christian Herdeg.

Die leichte, transparente Gestaltung der offenen Schalter unterstützt die fliessende Raumwirkung. Mit Rücksicht auf das stark farbige Lichtobjekt ist die Material- und Farbgebung dabei bewusst zurückhaltend gewählt.

The UBS wanted to improve substantially its presence on Claraplatz in Basel and enlarge its range of service counters and cash-points.

The existing floor plan, which is divided into two areas, is brought together to form a unified spatial experience with an arc of a circle. This effect is underscored by a skylight accommodating the round wall and a neon light sculpture by the artist Christian Herdeg.

The light, transparent design of the open counters enhances the sense of fluent space. The choice of materials and colours is consciously reticent to allow the highly coloured light sculpture to achieve maximum impact.

Grundriss 1:300
Ground plan 1:300

eigentlich auch können, oder wenigstens verstehen.

CF Könnt Ihr das an einem Beispiel Eurer Arbeit erklären?

DW Beim Wettbewerb Breite hat am Anfang jeder ein eigenes Projekt erarbeitet. Dann legten wir die drei Modelle auf den Tisch. Jeder war natürlich überzeugt von seinem Vorschlag. Das war sehr intensiv.

EB Am Anfang, als nur Timmy und ich zusammen gearbeitet haben, ging vieles schneller. Heute ist die Auseinandersetzung vor allem in der Entwurfsphase stärker und braucht mehr Verarbeitungszeit. Nach der Konzeptphase allerdings wird ein Projekt einem von uns zugeteilt: einer übernimmt also nach aussen die Verantwortung. Wir versuchen natürlich weiterhin, regelmässig Gespräche über das Projekt zu führen. Es liegt jedoch in der Initiative desjenigen, der die Verantwortung hat, die anderen dazuzuholen, was nicht immer einfach ist.

DW Man tendiert dazu, sie nur zu holen, wenn man Probleme hat.

TON Und nicht, wenn man nicht merkt, dass man eigentlich ein Problem hat...

EB Ich habe ausserdem das Gefühl, dass das Gespräch mit Daniel und anderen jungen Mitarbeitern zur Kritik ermutigt. Sie merken, wie wichtig es für uns ist, angriffig zu sein.

CF Und ist die räumliche Situation, die Ihr für Euer Büro gewählt habt, bewusst im Hinblick auf diese Kommunikation gewählt worden?

EB Ja, ganz klar.

Das Objekt und sein Kontext

CF Es erscheint mir charakteristisch für Euer Büro, dass viele Projekte hauptsächlich auf der städtebaulichen Ebene entwickelt

DW For the Breite competition we each developed a project of our own to start with. Then we put the three models on the table. Of course each one of us was completely committed to his own proposal. That was all very intense.

EB In the early days, when only Timmy and I were working together, things went a lot more quickly. Now there is much more discussion and analysis at the design stage and we need more time to process things. Certainly after the conceptual phase a project will be assigned to one of us: one person takes over responsibility as far as the outside world is concerned. Of course we continue to have regular discussions about the project. But it is up to the person who is in charge to bring the others in, and that is not always so simple.

DW One tends to bring them in only when one has problems.

TON And not when you don't notice that there actually is a problem ...

EB I also have a feeling that the discussion with Daniel and other young colleagues encourages criticism. They realize how important it is for us to be aggressive.

CF And the way you have arranged your office space must have been chosen for this sort of communication?

EB Yes, of course.

The object and its context

CF It seems to me to be typical of your office that many projects are developed mainly on the plane of urban development. I experienced this as a member of the jury for the PAX competition and also in the case of the Kantonalbank in Birsfelden. Here I am particu

Erweiterung der Hauptverwaltung in der
City Nord, Hamburg, TCHIBO Holding AG,
1986-1989
Extension of Headquarters in City Nord, Hamburg, TCHIBO Holding AG, 1986-1989

werden. Das habe ich als Mitglied des Preisgerichts beim PAX-Gebäude erlebt, aber auch bei der Kantonalbank in Birsfelden. Hier interessiert mich besonders der Hintergrund. Unsere Ausbildung – und da meine ich auch Euch, Timmy und Edi, – war sehr objektorientiert. Deshalb frage ich erst Dich, Daniel: Welche Bedeutung, meinst Du, hat bei Euren Arbeiten diese Integration des architektonischen Entwurfes in einen städtebaulichen Kontext?

DW Aus der Lektüre des Kontextes erarbeitet man sich Werkzeuge oder «Pflöcke» im Feld der Möglichkeiten. Entsprechend strukturiert man nachher die Aufgabe. Dies kann dazu führen, dass das Projekt ganz anderen Gesetzen folgt, als man auf den ersten Blick gedacht hat.

Ein Beispiel ist der Wettbewerb für das Freibad in Riehen: nachdem wir die Situation studiert hatten, kamen wir zur Auffassung, dass man möglichst wenig hinzufügen sollte. Wir schlugen vor, den Fluss «Wiese» als vorhandene, natürliche Grenze auch für die Begrenzung des Freigeländes zu nutzen.

CF Das sind für mich jetzt mehr Haltungen als Werkzeuge. Wenn Du vorher ‹Werkzeug› gesagt hast, was meintest Du damit?

DW Damals hatten wir gerade unser erstes Autocad-Programm am PC, und wir waren fasziniert von der Layerstruktur. Man kann mit Knopfdruck die Höhenlinien oder Flussläufe aus dem Zusammenhang isolieren. Das ermöglicht eine bestimmte Art des Se-

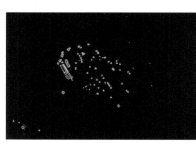

hens und der Analyse. Der PC war in diesem Fall das Werkzeug. In einem anderen Fall wäre es zum Beispiel ein Modell aus Ton. Man verwendet diese Hilfsmittel wie eine spezielle Brille oder einen Filter.

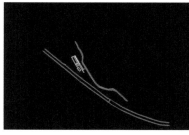

larly interested in the background. Our training – and I'm including you, Timmy and Edi, here – was very object-oriented. And so I'll ask you first, Daniel: what do you think is the importance of integrating an architectural design into an urban development context?

DW By reading the context we are able to establish tools or "pegs" in the field of possibilities. And then we structure the job correspondingly. This can also mean that the project follows quite different rules than one thought it would at first. Take the competition for the open-air swimming-pool in Riehen: after we had studied the site, we came to feel that as little as possible should be added. We suggested to use the river "Wiese" as an existing, natural boundary for the recreation area.

CF I see these more as attitudes than tools. When you said "tool" earlier what did you mean by it?

DW In this case we had just got our first Autocad program on the PC, and we were fascinated by the layer structure. You can isolate contours or river-beds at the touch of a button. This makes it possible to look and analyse in a particular way. Then the PC was the tool. Another time it could be a clay model. We use these aids like a pair of special spectacles or a filter.

CF And that means you adopt a particular point of view?

DW It means that we take the significance of these tools seriously. I see this as a way of avoiding formal thought for as long as possible. Working out criteria and strategies from the context before choosing the form.

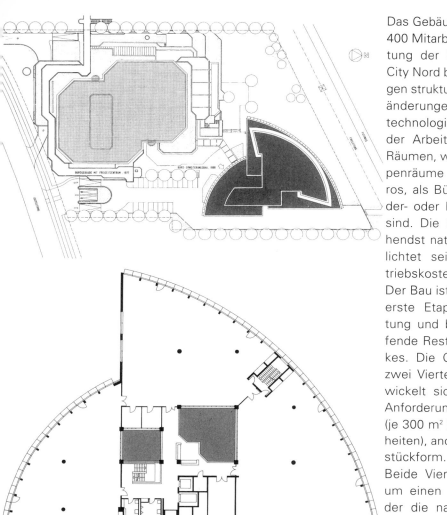

Das Gebäude bildet einen Teil (ca. 400 Mitarbeiter) der Hauptverwaltung der Firma TCHIBO in der City Nord bei Hamburg. Die häufigen strukturorganisatorischen Veränderungen der Firma und die technologischen Entwicklungen der Arbeitswelt verlangen nach Räumen, welche sowohl als Gruppenräume wie auch als Zellenbüros, als Büros wie auch als Sonder- oder Laborräume zu nutzen sind. Die Räume sollen weitgehendst natürlich belüftet und belichtet sein und minimale Betriebskosten aufweisen.

Der Bau ist angeschlossen an die erste Etappe der Hauptverwaltung und belegt die spitz zulaufende Restfläche des Grundstückes. Die Gebäudeform, die aus zwei Viertelkreisen besteht, entwickelt sich einerseits aus den Anforderungen der Gruppenbüros (je 300 m² bis 500 m² grosse Einheiten), anderseits aus der Grundstückform.

Beide Viertelkreise sind jeweils um einen Innenhof angeordnet, der die natürliche Durchlüftung der Büroräume ermöglicht. Diese Innenhöfe werden als Zwischenwelt empfunden: für die Mitarbeiter in den Büros als Aussenraum, für die Mitarbeiter, die im Gebäude unterwegs sind, als Innenraum. Sie bilden also eine Kommunikationszone quer durch den ganzen Bau.

The building forms a part (approximately 400 employees) of the TCHIBO headquarters in City Nord near Hamburg. Frequent changes of the firm's organizational structure and technological developments in the world of work require spaces that can be used as group spaces, and also as cell units, offices, specialist rooms or laboratories. The rooms should be naturally lit and ventilated to as large an extent as possible, and be inexpensive to run.

This building is attached to the TCHIBO headquarters erected during the first building phase, occupying the remainder of the site, which tapers to a point. The building is in the form of two quarter circles and develops from the need for group offices (300 m² to 500 m² large units), and also from the configuration of the plot.

The requirement for natural ventilation determined the design from the start. Thus both quarter circles are arranged around an inner courtyard which makes natural lateral ventilation of the office space possible. These inner courtyards are seen as an in-between world: as an outdoor space by the office workers and an indoor space by employees circulating in the building. They thus form a commu-

Situation 1:1800
Site plan 1:1800
Grundriss Normalgeschoss 1:650
Ground plan of normal floor 1:650

CF Dann wird daraus eine Haltung?

DW Die Haltung ist, dass man die Bedeutung dieser Werkzeuge ernst nimmt. Ich sehe darin eine Möglichkeit, möglichst lange nicht formal zu denken. Sich erst Kriterien und Strategien aus dem Kontext zu erarbeiten, bevor man die Form wählt.

CF Kann man das eine kontextuelle Haltung nennen?

DW Ja.

CF Und woher kommt sie bei Dir?

DW Die kommt daher, dass sehr vieles schon da ist.

CF Das ist nicht die Antwort auf meine Frage. Ist das eine Prägung aus deiner Reinkarnation heraus? Oder ist das etwas, was Du an der Schule erfahren hast?

DW An der Architectural Association wurden den Studenten keine Entwurfsaufgaben gestellt. Wir hatten kein Raumprogramm und meistens auch keinen vorgegebenen Ort. Der Student musste die Gründe für das, was er tat, selber suchen. Um auf deine Frage zu antworten: Ja, ich glaube, dass dadurch jeder Student gezwungen wurde, über den Kontext seiner Arbeit nachzudenken. Ich habe zum Beispiel damals für die Insel Skyros ein Haus mit einem fliegenden Dach entwickelt. Dieser Ansatz hat sich erst ergeben, als ich herausfand, dass der Wind für die Kultur der Insel seit Jahrtausenden eine zentrale Rolle spielt.

TON Man muss den Begriff Kontext sehr weit fassen: Es gibt einen sozialen Kontext, einen Verkehrs-Kontext, einen volumetrischen, es gibt auch einen historischen Kontext, sogar einen Prozess-Kontext, der etwa zeigt, in welcher Entwicklungsphase ein Stadtquartier ist. Die Idee des Grossraumbüros zum Beispiel muss man in einem sozialen und

CF And can that then be called a contextual attitude?

DW Yes.

CF And where does it come from in your case?

DW It comes from the fact that a great deal is already there.

CF That does not answer my question. Is that an imprint left by your reincarnation? Or is it something you learned at school?

DW Students were not given design exercises at the Architectural Association. No specific framework was laid down. Students had to find their own reasons for what they were doing. To answer your question, yes, I think that this made every student think about the context of his or her work. For example, I designed a house with a flying roof for the island of Skyros at that time. The design didn't occur to me until I discovered that wind had played a central role in the island's culture for thousands of years.

TON The notion of context has to be addressed very broadly: there is a social context, a transport context, a volumetric one, there is also a historic context, even a process context, that can show the current state of development in a particular neighbourhood. For example, the idea of an open-plan office has to be seen in a social and an economic context.

It is only when you have tried to read an idea with a wide variety of filters that "surpluses" and "shortfalls" are revealed.

CF Can you explain that in terms of a piece of work?

TON Take the Breite competition, for example. As far as defining this site is concerned the place is a gap; but it is also a gap as far as noise is concerned and in terms of movement and

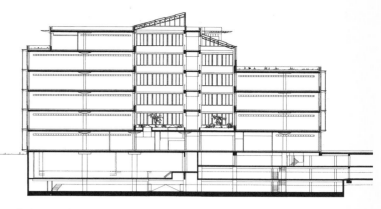

Die Gebäudeform, die genaue Ausgestaltung der Höfe sowie Lage und Grösse der Fenster wurden anhand von Windkanalversuchen mit Modellen 1:130 (Gebäudemodell) und 1:10 (Geschossmodell) überprüft respektive entwickelt. So konnten die spezifischen Witterungsverhältnisse in Hamburg (Windböen etc.) möglichst präzise simuliert werden. Vor der definitiven Gestaltung des abgehängten Akustikrasters und der Anordnung der Lüftungskanäle wurde ein weiterer Versuch im Massstab 1:1 durchgeführt.

An die Innenhöfe angrenzend und über sie belichtet sind die offenen Vertikalverbindungen und die Pausenzonen der einzelnen Geschosse.

Für die künstliche Beleuchtung wurde eigens ein Beleuchtungskörper entwickelt, der den Ansprüchen der Variabilität der Raumgliederung und den besonderen lüftungstechnischen Anforderungen gerecht wird.

nication zone running right through the whole building.

The shape of the building, the precise design of the courtyards and the positioning and size of the windows were tested and developed using wind tunnel experiments with a building model (1:130) and a floor model (1:10). This made it possible to simulate the specific Hamburg weather conditions (gusts of wind etc.) as specifically as possible. Another experiment was conducted on a 1:1 scale for the final design of the suspended acoustic grid and the arrangement of the ventilation ducts.

The open vertical links and the leisure areas for the individual floors are adjacent to the inner courtyards and lit from them.

A light fixture was specially developed to meet the artificial light needs arising from the variable spatial structure and the particular technical ventilation requirements.

Schnitt durch den Lichthof 1:750
Section through the atrium 1:750
Rauchstudie zur Klärung der natürlichen Durchlüftung
Smoke study to investigate natural ventilation

einem wirtschaftlichen Kontext sehen.

Erst wenn man versucht hat, eine Aufgabe mit den verschiedensten Filtern zu lesen, zeigen sich «Überhänge» und «Unterhänge».

CF Kannst Du das anhand einer Arbeit erklären?

TON Zum Beispiel der Wettbewerb in der Breite. Der Ort ist, was die Definition dieses Geviertes anbelangt, eine Lücke; er ist aber auch, was Lärm anbelangt, eine Lücke und ebenso, was Bewegung und Abschirmung von Bewegung anbelangt. Er ist aus sehr vielen verschiedenen Perspektiven eine Lücke. Das nenne ich einen Unterhang, der gefüllt werden will.

Aussenraum

CF In meinen 14 Jahren als Bauherr in Basel bestand mein Engagement hauptsächlich darin, die Architekten dazu zu zwingen, kontextuell zu denken. Ich meine, die Preise haben diejenigen Büros gewonnen, die das gemacht haben. Mit Ausnahme von Mario Botta, wo ich überstimmt wurde. Aber beim Rosshof, bei den Baulücken Spalenvorstadt und Schützenmattstrasse, bei der Breite, der PAX, der Bâloise und dem Picasso-Platz wurde in den Preisgerichten die Diskussion um den Kontext geführt. Die engere Wahl wurde meist auf der Ebene des städtebaulichen Entwurfes getroffen. War das bei Eurem Projekt für Muttenz ähnlich?

TON Ich meine ja. Unsere erste Aussage war es, einen Platz zu bilden, der an die Hauptstrasse anschliesst. Von diesem Platz aus konnten wir den ganzen Entwurf aufrollen.

DW Und dort lag das Problem vor allem in der Typologie: Wie integriert man einen «Fladen» von 2500 m² Erdgeschossfläche

protection from movement. I[t] is a gap in a large number o[f] respects. I call that a shortfal[l] that has to be redressed.

Exterior space

CF In my 14 years as Director o[f] Hochbauamt in Basel I wa[s] above all committed to forcing architects to think in context. [I] think that the prizes went t[o] the offices who did that. Wit[h] the exception of Mario Botta: [I] was outvoted there. But in th[e] case of the Rosshof, the buildin[g] gaps in the Spalenvorstadt an[d] Schützenmattstrasse, the Breit[e] project, the PAX, the Bâloise an[d] the Picasso-Platz the juries' di[s]cussions revolved around context. The short list was usuall[y] drawn up on the qualification[s] in urban design. Were thing[s] similar for your Muttenz pro[ject?

TON I think so. Our first state[ment was that we would build [a] square that joined up with th[e] main street. We were able to de[ve]lop the whole of the design out from the square as a nucle[us...

DW And there the problem wa[s] above all one of typology: ho[w] does one integrate 2500 m² [of] "pancake" into a village? The typ[i]cal flat-footed building proble[m]

TON Or reservoir problem.

DW We decided to cut off th[e] base flush with the high-ris[e] buildings, so that they linke[d] the base with the flatness of i[ts] surroundings.

CF Re-evaluating exterior urba[n] space is as important as the di[a]logue with existing urba[n] structures: the architectural de[sign and its external space must relate to the existing si[tu]ation. Was the case in Bir[felden similar to that in Mu[t]tenz?

TON There too the typologic[al

Fernmeldezentrum Basel-Grosspeter,
Generaldirektion PTT, 1984-1989
**Basel-Grosspeter Telecommunications
Centre, PTT Headquarters, 1984-1989**

in ein Dorf? Das typische Platt-
fussgebäude-Problem.

TON Oder Stausee-Problem.

DW Wir haben uns entschieden, den Sockel mit den Hochbauten überall bündig abzuschneiden. So binden die Hochbauten den Sockel in seine Umgebung ein.

CF Neben dem Dialog mit vorhandenen städtebaulichen Strukturen ist auch die Neubewertung des städtischen Aussenraumes wichtig: Dass der architektonische Entwurf mit seinen Aussenräumen in Bezug auf die vorhandene Situation gedacht wird. War das in Birsfelden ähnlich wie in Muttenz?

TON Da war auch der Typologiekampf das Entscheidende.

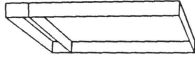

DW Eigentlich auch wieder das Problem des Breitfusses. Die Erdgeschossfläche war wieder grösser als die Hochbaufläche. Wir waren im Wettbewerb die einzigen, die zwei Bauten vorgeschlagen haben: ein dreigeschossiges und ein eingeschossiges Gebäude.

CF Trotzdem scheint mir die Qualität dieses Entwurfes ganz wesentlich die Stufung des öffentlichen Raumes, seine Hierarchie und Dimensionierung zu sein.

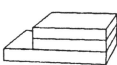

DW Das war die Absicht: Gerade durch die Trennung in zwei Baukörper kann jedes Volumen für sich eine präzise Rolle im städtischen Raum spielen: das dreigeschossige zur Strasse hin, das eingeschossige zum Zentrumsplatz. Die Hierarchie der Zwischenräume hatten wir schon im Wettbewerbsbericht illustriert.

Die Angst vor der Form

CF Jetzt interessiert mich noch eine Äusserung von Dir, Daniel: zum Versuch, möglichst lange nicht formal zu werden. Heisst das, dass die Form des Gebäudes wie von selber entsteht? Oder ist die Form anonym und nicht be-

struggle was crucial.

DW Actually is was the broad foot problem again. The ground floor area was again bigger tha[n] the high-rise volume. We wer[e] the only ones in the competi tion to suggest two buildings: [a] three-storey and single-store[y] building.

CF Nevertheless it seems to m[e] that the quality of this desig[n] lies very much in the gradatio[n] of the public space, its hierar chy and dimensions.

DW That was the intention: it i[s] precisely because the projec[t] was divided into two building[s] that each volume is able to pla[y] a precise role in the urba[n] space: the three-storey buildin[g] on the street side and the sin gle storey building relating t[o] the central square. We alread[y] illustrated the hierarchy of th[e] spaces in-between in our com petition report.

Fear of form

CF Now I'd like to take up some thing you said, Daniel, abou[t] the attempt to resist becomin[g] formal for as long as possibl[e] Does that mean that the for[m] of a building emerges of it[s] own accord? Or is form ano nymous and not conscious Where does this fear of the fo[r] mal concept come from?

DW I think that one's work i[s] often self-referential: one con stantly falls back on one's favou rite formal images. The searc[h] for something particular ough[t] to be free from these persona[l] preferences to as far as po[s] sible.

CF Can you give an example [of] that?

TON Let me try. The castle i[n] Karlsruhe is semicircular, bu[t] not for formal reasons. Th[e] main impetus behind the de sign was security. Sufficient u[n]

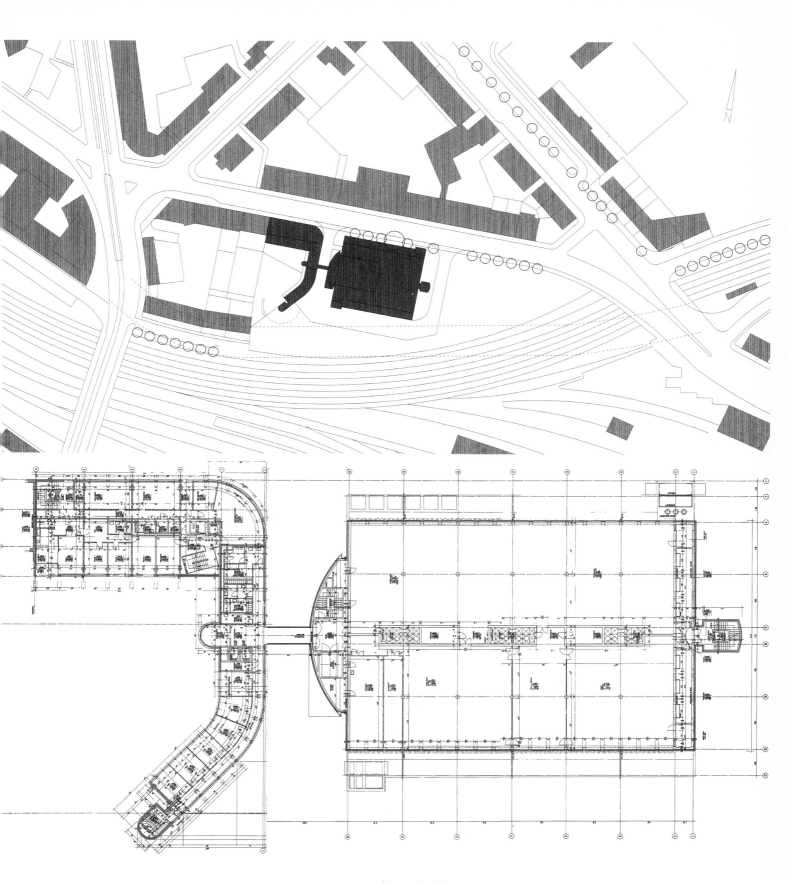

Situation 1:2100
Site plan 1:2100
Grundriss 2. Obergeschoss 1:500
2nd floor ground plan 1:500

wusst? Woher kommt diese Angst vor dem formalen Konzept?

DW Ich glaube, dass man sich oft selber zitiert. Dabei verfällt man immer wieder in die gleichen formalen Lieblingsbilder. Die Suche nach dem Eigen-Artigen sollte möglichst frei von diesen persönlichen Vorlieben sein.

CF Kannst Du das an einem Beispiel erklären?.

TON Darf ich ein Beispiel zu geben versuchen? Das Karlsruher Schloss ist nicht aus formalen Gründen halbkreisförmig. Die Triebfeder dazu war eine Frage der Sicherheit. Man wollte über eine gewisse Strecke ungehindert auf angreifendes Volk schiessen können.

CF Das ist Deine Interpretation. Aber das Schloss ist natürlich auch ein Bild des absolutistischen Herrschers.

TON Eben, Distanz halten.

CF Distanz halten, ja. Aber auch ein monumentales Abbild der zentralistischen Staatsidee. Ähnlich wie der ägyptische Pharao, der in einer Pyramide draussen vor der Stadt begraben wurde.

TON Beide Beispiele sind ähnlich in der Monumentalisierung des Herrschens, haben aber formal einen ganz verschiedenen Ausdruck. Die gleiche Triebfeder hat an einem anderen Standort zu einer anderen, ebenso schönen Lösung geführt.
Aber wenn man die Form des Halbkreises einfach übernimmt, ohne diese Triebfeder, dann geht immer etwas von ihrem Reichtum verloren.

CF Willst du damit unterstellen, dass Ihr so miese Architekten seid, dass Ihr Formalismen in Euren Köpfen habt und die unreflektiert anwendet?

DW Ich glaube, man neigt sehr schnell dazu.

TON Wir dürfen hier nicht nur über die Form diskutieren. Archi-

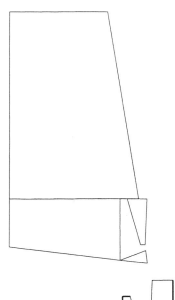

obstructed terrain was needed to fire on intruders.

CF That is your interpretation. But the castle also symbolizes absolute authority.

TON Exactly, keep your distance.

CF Keep your distance, yes. But it is also a monumental image of the centralist state idea. Rather like the Egyptian Pharaoh who was buried in a pyramid outside the town.

TON Both these examples are similar in that they monumentalize the ruling process, but formally they are expressed quite differently. Different solution in different locations, but equally beautiful.
But if you adopt a semicircular form without this compelling force, then something of it richness is always lost.

CF Are you insinuating that you are such rotten architects that you have formal ideas in your heads and use them without thinking?

DW I think that one very quickly inclines to that.

TON We should not just discuss form here. Architecture always addresses all human senses. For example, a new living space always penetrates all the senses from sight to touch to smell. The more complete this chain is the richer is the experience. Today one often tends to exaggerate only the visual impression. Then there is a danger that only visual criteria are used for the design.

CF All your arguments about form sound very rational to me. I think there is no such thing as innocent forms. They can be dull or intense, but they are never innocent, but implementations of value judgements. So when I draw a straight line I am trying to create order, when

Das Grundstück liegt in einer stark lärmbelasteten Umgebung, die fast ausnahmslos Wohn- oder Wohn-/Bürocharakter aufweist. Das umfangreiche Raumprogramm verlangte nach erweiterbaren Betriebsräumen für Telekommunikationsanlagen sowie nach Büroräumen mit Besprechungszonen und Infrastruktur.

Um die beiden Funktionen der Anlage nach aussen lesbar zu machen, wurde das beträchtliche Bauvolumen in zwei Baukörper gegliedert: einen «Menschentrakt» mit Büros und Wohnungen und einen «Maschinentrakt» mit den technischen Räumen für Telekommunikation.

Der «Menschentrakt» übernimmt die Höhe und Gliederung der angrenzenden Wohnbebauung. Er ist im Vergleich zum «Maschinentrakt» in seiner Geometrie freier und umschliesst einen Gartenhof, auf den hin alle wichtigen Funktionen orientiert sind.

Der «Maschinentrakt» setzt sich von der Strassenflucht ab, markiert quasi den Anfang einer neuen Industriezone und schafft einen neuen, grossen Massstab. Um eine grösstmögliche Flexibilität im Inneren zu erhalten, wird ein Grossteil der Ver- und Entsorgungsinfrastruktur ausserhalb der eigentlichen Gebäudehülle geführt.

Die beiden unterschiedlichen Welten sind durch Brücken miteinander verbunden, und somit auch die beiden angrenzenden Quartiere: das Wohnquartier im Westen und das «neue» Industriequartier im Osten.

The site is in a very noise-polluted area of almost entirely residential or residential/office character. The extensive planning requirements asked for extendible areas for telecommunications equipment and office space with conference rooms and infrastructure.

In order to make the complex's two functions intelligible from outside, the considerable volume was divided into two buildings: a "human section" with offices and housing and a "machine section" with technical telecommunications spaces.

The "human section" adopts the height and articulation of the adjacent residential development. Its geometry is freer than that of the "machine section" and includes a garden courtyard on to which all the important functions face.

The "machine section" detaches itself from the street line, effectively marking the beginning of a new industrial zone and creating a new, large scale. In order to achieve the greatest possible flexibility in the interior a large part of the supply and disposal infrastructure is mounted outside the actual skin of the building.

These two different worlds are connected by bridges, and thus the two adjacent quarters as well: the western residential quarter and the "new" industrial quarter in the east.

tektur spricht immer den ganzen Menschen an. Ein neuer Wohnraum zum Beispiel geht seinen Weg durch alle Sinne: durch das Visuelle über das Haptische bis zum Geruch. Je vollständiger diese Kette ist, desto reicher ist das Erlebnis. Heute tendiert man oft dazu, nur den optischen Eindruck zu bewerten. Dann besteht die Gefahr, nur nach optischen Kriterien zu entwerfen.

CF Eure ganze Argumentation um die Form klingt für mich sehr rational. Für mich gibt es keine unschuldigen Formen. Sie können dumpf oder intensiv sein, aber sie sind nie unschuldig, sondern sie sind Umsetzungen von Werthaltungen. Also wenn ich eine gerade Linie zeichne, will ich Ordnung schaffen, wenn ich eine krumme Linie zeichne, will ich Unordnung verbreiten.

TON Diese Haltung stimmt nicht immer. Ich kann mir vorstellen, in gewissen Situationen ist eine Kurve ordnender als eine Gerade.

CF Aber jede Form ist doch bestimmt von einem Willen zur Gestaltgebung, im Hinblick auf ein Bild.

DW In unserer Arbeit steht dieses Bild selten am Anfang. Je länger man warten kann mit der Formulierung eines Bildes, desto interessanter wird es. Ein Lieb-

lingsbeispiel von mir ist der Briefkasten. Wenn man die Aufgabe erhält, einen Briefkasten zu entwerfen, kommen einem gleich etliche Bilder in den Sinn. Egal, ob aus Schmiedeeisen, Holz oder Aluminium, schon ist man im formalen Denken. Während jemand, der sich erst einmal die Türe anschaut, nur ein bisschen Farbe braucht.

CF Da müssten wir noch grosse Bogen fahren, wenn wir jetzt da weitermachen wollten.

TON Nein, bleiben wir trotzdem. Beim Wettbewerb für das Freibad

draw a crooked line I want to spread disorder.

TON This attitude is not always correct. I can imagine that in certain circumstances a curve can create more order than a straight line.

CF But surely every form is determined by the will to create shape, with a view to an image.

DW In our work this image is rarely the first thing we address. The longer you can wait before formulating an image the more interesting it becomes. One of my favourite examples is the letter-box. If you are commissioned to design a letter box then all kinds of ideas flood into your mind. It doesn't matter whether it's wrought iron, wood or aluminium, you are already thinking formally. While someone who is just looking at the door needs a little bit of paint.

CF We'd have to make quite a detour to get any further in that direction.

TON No, let's keep at it. For the Riehen open-air swimming-pool competition we placed a building perpendicular to the slope. Because the hill is called "Schlipf", and indeed does "slip" all the time, the building is supported on two piers anchored in the rock. The hill can slide through underneath. Here too the form of the building did not emerge from an existing image but developed from observation of the context. The building is intended to refer more to the moving mountain than to itself.

CF And that is conscious form giving, isn't it?

TON That is conscious form-finding. There is a slight difference, I think.

CF Are you afraid of the cliché in your heads?

Verwaltungsneubau am Aeschenplatz,
Basel, PAX Schweizerische Lebens-
versicherungsgesellschaft, 1989-1997
Office Building on Aeschenplatz, Basel,
PAX Schweizerische Lebensver-
sicherungsgesellschaft, 1989-1997

in Riehen haben wir ein Gebäude quer zum Hang gestellt. Da der Berg Schlipf heisst und tatsächlich kontinuierlich «schlipft», steht das Gebäude auf zwei Pfeilern, die in den Fels gebohrt sind. Der Berg kann unten durchrutschen. Auch hier ist die Form des Gebäudes nicht aus einem vorhandenen Bild entstanden, sondern hat sich aus der Beobachtung des Kontextes entwickelt. Das Haus soll auf den wandernden Berg verweisen und weniger auf sich selbst.

CF Und das ist jetzt bewusste Formgebung, oder?

TON Das ist bewusste Formfindung. Da, meine ich, ist ein kleiner Unterschied.

CF Habt ihr Angst vor den Klischees, die in Eurem Kopf sind?

DW Ja. Glücklicherweise existieren für zeitgemässe Aufgaben solche Klischees oft gar nicht. Für die Gestaltung der Geldautomatenwand einer Bank gibt es keine Archetypen. In der Regel werden hier vorhandene Archetypen auf eine neue Aufgabenstellung aufgesetzt, indem man die Wand mit Chromstahl, Holzkassetten oder Granit verkleidet.
Bei der Gestaltung dieser Wand in Birsfelden haben wir den Schlüssel für die Gestaltung im Charakter der Automaten gesucht, ihrem ephemerischen «Datennebel». Daraus ist die Idee entstanden, die Wand aus Mattglas zu machen. Künstler sollten dann eingeladen werden, um Bilder von hinten an diese Wand zu projezieren. Ihre Gestalt sollte so ephemerisch sein wie ihr Inhalt, die elektronischen Daten.

Ausbildung, Vorbilder

CF Edi und Timmy, ich glaube, in der Ausbildung Eurer Generation waren die Bilder und Mythen klar. Man hat nur nach der Perfektionierung dieser Mythen

DW Yes. Fortunately there aren't any clichés like that for contemporary problems. There are no archetypes for designing a wall of cash-points for a bank. As a rule, existing archetypes are applied to a new problem by cladding the wall with chrome steel, timber coffering or granite.
When designing this wall in Birsfelden we looked for the key to the design in the character of the machines, their ephemeral "data fog". This gave us the idea of making the wall of frosted glass. Artists were then to be invited to project pictures onto this wall from behind. Their appearance was to be as ephemeral as their content, the electronic data.

Training, models

CF Edi and Timmy, I think that when your generation studied the images and myths were clear. People just sought to perfect these myths. For this reason they concentrated on structural-technical and functional matters.

EB Yes, very much so. In the fifties, when I finished my studies and started to practise, the technical developments were enormous.

CF But the converse can also be true: technical development was so rapid because of limitations in terms of content.

EB That's right. We were confronted with very complex technical problems in our early activities. A large part of our early professional practice consisted of trying to harmonize function, technology and construction to the greatest possible extent. The design aspect was not so much isolated in the foreground as it is today.

DW The images behind the de

Die besondere Lage des Grundstücks stellte vor allem die Frage nach einem städtebaulichen Abschluss für den Aeschenplatz, einem räumlich nur schwer definierbaren Verkehrsknotenpunkt im Bereich des ehemaligen «Aeschentors». Das Projekt führt den ehemaligen Grabenraum weiter und versucht so, den Platz auf seinen Kernbereich zu fokussieren: Der Standort wird also in erster Linie nicht als Platzabschluss, sondern als Ort zwischen zwei ungleichwertigen, zusammenlaufenden Strassenzügen verstanden. Die angrenzenden Strassenräume der St. Alban-Anlage und der Malzgasse werden beide mit mural gehaltenen, verklinkerten Bauten begleitet. Ihre Verschiedenartigkeit – Ringstrasse einerseits und Vorstadtgasse andererseits – wird mit stark unterschiedlichen Gebäudehöhen beantwortet, in der zweigeschossigen Aussenhalle werden sie am Aeschenplatz zusammengeführt.

The special position of the site raised the particular question of an urban conclusion for Aeschenplatz, which is a traffic junction, somewhat difficult to define in spatial terms, in the area of the former "Aeschen Gate". The project continues the line of the former defensive ditch and in this way tries to focus the square on its core area: thus the site is not primarily perceived as the end of the square, but as a place between two converging streets of different status. The adjacent street spaces of the St. Alban-Anlage and Malzgasse are both accompanied by brick structures retaining the character of a wall. Their different natures – one is a ring road and the other a suburban alleyway – are responded to by very different building heights, and they are brought together on Aeschenplatz in the two-storey outer hall.

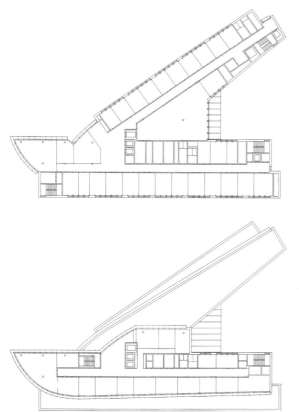

Situation 1:4200
Site plan 1:4200
Grundriss Erdgeschoss 1:950
Ground plan 1:950
Grundriss Normalgeschoss 1:950
Normal floor 1:950
Grundriss Dachgeschoss 1:950
Roof storey 1:950

gesucht. Deshalb hat man sich auf das Konstruktiv-Technische und Funktionale konzentriert.

EB Ja, sehr stark. In den fünfziger Jahren, als ich vom Studium in die Praxis kam, war die technische Entwicklung enorm.

CF Es kann aber auch umgekehrt sein: aufgrund der inhaltlichen Beschränkung war die technische Entwicklung so rasch.

EB Ja, richtig. In unserer frühen Tätigkeit waren wir mit technisch sehr komplexen Projekten konfrontiert. Ein Grossteil unserer ersten Berufspraxis bestand darin, Funktion, Technik und Konstruktion möglichst perfekt in Einklang zu bringen. Der gestalterische Aspekt stand dabei nicht so gesondert im Vordergrund wie heute.

DW Die Bilder, die der Gestaltung zugrunde lagen, sind nicht in Frage gestellt worden?

EB Nein.

CF Mir scheint es interessant, dass in unserer Generation nie über die Idee der Form gesprochen wurde. Ein Prinzip war heilig gesprochen und seine Infragestellung tabuisiert: «form follows function», die konstruktive Idee muss ablesbar sein, und eine andere Idee als die konstruktive gibt es nicht.

TON Ich war im Umbruch. Ich war ja zwei Jahre bei Hoesli: «Jetzt Herr Fischer, wo ist Ihre Idee?»

CF Ja, der Hoesli hat in der Schweiz diesen Umbruch gebracht.

EB In meiner Generation sind wir indoktriniert worden mit Funktion und der «konstruktiven Wahrheit».

CF Vor allem der Glaube an die Wahrheit ist hier bemerkenswert. Welches sind die ältesten Bürgin & Nissen Bauten in diesem Buch?

EB Das Fernmeldegebäude am Grosspeter und Tchibo.

sign were not questioned?

EB No.

CF It seems interesting to me that our generation never spoke about the idea of form. One principle had been sanctified and any questioning of it was taboo: "form follows function", the structural idea must be intelligible, and there is no other idea than the structural one.

TON I came in when it was already changing. I was under Hoesli for two years: "Well, Mister Fischer, where's your idea?"

CF Yes, Hoesli did bring about this change in Switzerland.

EB In my generation we were indoctrinated with function and "structural truth".

CF It's the belief in truth that's the most remarkable thing here. What are the earliest Bürgin and Nissen buildings in this book?

EB The Grosspeter telecommunications building and Tchibo.

CF Are these buildings driven by archetypal ideas or more by this truth?

EB In the case of Tchibo, the two semicircles arose from the shape of the site and the fact that natural ventilation was required. No claim to truth, but clearly directed towards function.

TON In the case of the telecommunications building I would give a mixed reply. It's certainly true that the spatial programme variously serves "machine building" and "people building", but this division also reflects the urban surroundings.

CF Now, in comparison with this approach, where did the idea of the Sierpinsky cube for the Breite competition come from? I see that much more as a formal concept.

DW As Timmy mentioned above the idea of the gap or the cavit

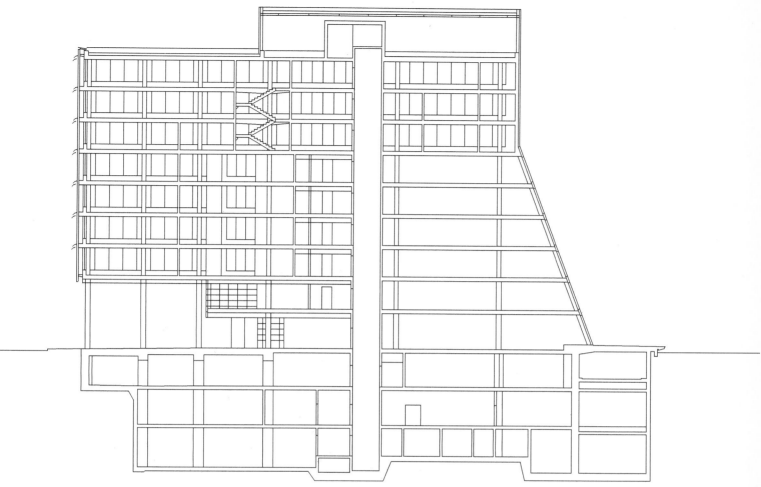

Der Verlauf des Baukörpers an der Malzgasse verzichtet darauf, dem Knick der Gasse zu folgen. Die Hauptrichtung der Gasse wird weitergeführt, bis sie dem Verlauf der St. Alban-Anlage begegnet. So wird die Geometrie der bedeutenderen Strasse, der St. Alban-Anlage, bis in die Malzgasse spürbar gestaltet. Um die Begegnung beider Strassen zu verdeutlichen, werden ihre Hauptrichtungen in der zweigeschossigen Aussenhalle des Baukörpers zum Aeschenplatz hin zusammengeführt. Die inneren Zonen der beiden Gebäudeflügel werden in ihrer Höhe hinter den muralen Baukörpern gestaffelt und in volumetrisch freieren, zweischichtig verglasten Baukörpern eingefasst.

The section of the building running along Malzgasse does not pick up the bend in the street. It follows the alley's main direction until it meets the line of the St. Alban-Anlage. Thus the geometry of the more important street, the St. Alban-Anlage, is unmistakably projected on to Malzgasse. In order to make the meeting of these two streets clearer, their main directions are brought together in the two-storey outer hall of the building on the Aeschenplatz side. The inner zones of the two wings of the building are staggered in height behind the parts of the building deliberately styled as walls, and are framed in volumetrically freer, double-layered glazed buildings.

Schnitt 1:400
Section 1:400

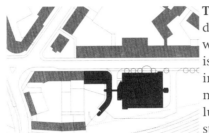

CF Sind diese Bauten von arche-typischen Ideen oder mehr von dieser Wahrheit geprägt?

EB Bei Tchibo sind die beiden Halbkreise aus der Form des Grundstückes und der Forderung nach natürlicher Lüftung ent-standen. Kein Anspruch auf Wahrheit, aber eine klare Orien-tierung an der Funktion.

TON Beim Fermeldegebäude wür-de ich eine durchmischte Ant-wort geben. Das Raumprogramm ist zwar nach seinen Funktionen in «Menschenhaus» und «Maschi-nenhaus» aufgeteilt, diese Auftei-lung reflektiert jedoch auch das städtebauliche Umfeld.

CF Wo kam nun im Vergleich zu diesen Ansätzen die Idee vom Sierpinsky-Würfel beim Wettbe-werb in der Breite her? In meinen Augen ist das eher ein formales Konzept.

DW Wie Timmy schon erwähnt hat, war der Begriff der Lücke, oder des Hohlraumes, sehr wich-tig. Allein schon der Rhein und die Autobahn sind zwei grosse Schneisen in der Stadt. Dies setzt sich im städtebaulich vorgegebe-nen Innenhof und im Raumpro-gramm mit seinen Ausstellungs-hallen fort. In der Verzahnung dieser Leerräume sahen wir ein grosses Potential: dass man zum Beispiel von der Ausstellungshal-le her gleichzeitig die Autobahn und den Rhein erlebt.

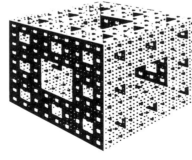

Dieser Ansatz hat uns an den Sierpinsky-Würfel erinnert: das absurde Objekt, welches eigent-lich ein Volumen ist, aber mit un-endlich viel Hohlraum. So wurde er zur Leitlinie für dieses Projekt. Besonders interessiert hat mich persönlich dabei, dass die Leit-linie nicht aus dem Bereich der Architektur kam. Architektur also nicht sich selber zitiert.

CF Könnte es auch sein, dass Du, weil Du der Bedeutung der Idee im formalen Bereich so viel Wich-

was very important. The Rhine and the motorway already cut two swathes through the city. This is continued in the inner courtyard, which is prescribed by the urban surroundings and the programme with its exhibi-tion areas. We saw a great po-tential in linking these empty spaces together: for example you can experience the motor-way and the Rhine at the same time from the exhibition hall. This approach reminded us of the Sierpinsky cube: that absurd object, which is actually a volu-me, but with an infinite am-ount of empty space. That is how it became a leitmotif for this project. I was personally inter-ested particularly in the fact that the guideline did not come from the realms of architec-ture. Thus architecture is not quoting itself.

CF Could it also be that you tend to get frightened when you have to define form because it becomes so important: you at-tach a great deal of importance to ideas in the field of form?

DW It's quite possible that this is what makes me so careful.

CF Function can be interpreted very individually as well. I re-member that I recently read that, in the context of Russian town planning in the thirties, someone once said that a bed could only be 60 cm wide. This was linked with the idea of so-ciety: modern people sleep in a bed that is only 60 cm wide.

TON Something that I call the "Zurich School": in the fifties they conceived their residential buildings so precisely that even the beds were made of concrete.

CF Conscious exclusion of the sensual comes into it as well. And the fact that Alfred Roth could say of the Weissenhof de-velopment: "Modern people

tigkeit gibst, dann Angst kriegst, die Form zu definieren, weil sie so wichtig wird?

DW Schon möglich, dass daher die Vorsicht kommt.

CF Auch die Funktion kann sehr stark individuell interpretiert werden. Ich erinnere mich, kürzlich habe ich über den russischen Städtebau in den dreissiger Jahren gelesen, dass einer gesagt hat, ein Bett dürfe nur 60 cm breit sein. Das hing mit der Idee der Gesellschaft zusammen: Der moderne Mensch schläft in einem Bett, das nur 60 cm breit ist.

TON Was ich die ‹Zürcher Schule› nenne: Die haben in den fünfziger Jahren ihre Wohnbauten so präzis konzipiert, dass sogar die Betten betoniert waren.

CF Auch die bewusste Ausklammerung des Sinnlichen. Dass Alfred Roth über die Weissenhofsiedlung sagen konnte: «Der moderne Mensch stinkt nicht, deshalb kann man ein Badezimmer in den Wohnraum entlüften.»

TON Das habe ich vorhin mit dem Weg durch die Sinne gemeint. Wenn die Sinne nicht durchgehend gepflegt werden, gibt es einen Bruch in der Kontinuität von abstrakter Triebfeder und gelebtem Eindruck.

CF Bleiben wir noch bei der Frage der Bilder. Wir haben diskutiert, dass es in den fünziger, sechziger und siebziger Jahren prägende Bilder dafür gab, wie die Gesellschaft sich in der Architektur und im Städtebau manifestieren will. Seither hat jedoch eine radikale Verunsicherung eingesetzt. Daniel, kannst Du sagen, wie das vor Deinem Hintergrund ist. Hattest Du das Gefühl, als Du in dieses Büro gekommen bist, dass Du etablierte Bilder in Frage stellen musst?

DW In erster Linie war es ein Kulturschock anderer Art. In London haben wir viel an der Auf-

don't stink, so you can ventilat« a bathroom into the living area.

TON That is what I meant before by running through th« senses. If the senses are no« constantly attended to there i« a break in the continuity o« abstract driving force and live« impression.

CF Let us stay with the questio« of images. We have touched o« the fact that in the fifties, six« ties and seventies there was a« abundance of key images t« show how society wanted t« appear in terms of architectur« and urban development. Bu« since then a radical sense of ir« security has set in. Daniel, ca« you say how that looks fror« your background? Did you fee« that you were having to que« tion established images whe« you joined this office?

DW Generally speaking it was« cultural shock of a differen« kind. In London we had done« great deal of work on breakin« down habitual categories in th« city. For example, at Liverpoo« Station, pig farmers and circu« tents are settling in between th« company headquarters again. In Basel this is not the case.« don't know why it is, but her« the world is still intact. A stree« is still a street, a square is« square.

CF What did that mean to you« Did you have to adapt? It mus« have been both things at firs« you had to contribute som« thing, but you also had to a« cept some givens as well.

DW As it was also the start « my professional career I expe« ienced coming to terms wit« the outside world much mor« acutely than anything that ha« pened between us as partners.« feel that we are still in a tra« sitional phase here. It is pe« haps a central point that whe«

lösung von gewohnten Kategorien in der Stadt gearbeitet. Bei Liverpool Station zum Beispiel siedeln sich zwischen Firmensitzen wieder Schweinebauern und Zirkuszelte an.

In Basel ist das nicht der Fall. Ich weiss nicht woran es liegt, aber hier herrscht noch die heile Welt. Eine Strasse ist noch eine Strasse, ein Platz noch ein Platz.

CF Was hat das für Dich bedeutet? Musstest Du Dich anpassen?

Am Anfang war es ja beides: einerseits musstest Du etwas einbringen, andererseits musstest Du etwas übernehmen.

DW Da es gleichzeitig der Anfang meiner Berufstätigkeit war, erlebte ich die Auseinandersetzung nach aussen viel stärker als zwischen uns Partnern. Nach meinem Gefühl sind wir hier immer noch in einer Übergangsphase. Ein zentraler Punkt ist vielleicht, dass ich mit Idee nicht immer das gleiche meine wie Edi und Timmy. Der Unterschied liegt wohl darin, dass ich die Idee eher ausserhalb der direkten Funktion eines Projektes ansiedle. Der Gedanke des Strichcodes bei der Coop-Fassade oder der Sierpinsky-Würfel in der Breite haben zwar mit der Funktion des Gebäudes zu tun, es gibt sie jedoch auch ohne das Gebäude. Sie sind irgendwie selbständig.

TON Was Vor- und Nachteile in beide Richtungen mit sich bringt. Sicher kann eine abstrakte Idee einem Projekt Kraft verleihen. Manchmal entwickelt sich die Idee jedoch zu unabhängig vom Projekt selbst. Hier muss man sehr sorgfältig prüfen, ob die Idee unter den gegebenen Umständen überhaupt umsetzbar ist. Erst kürzlich haben wir zum Beispiel versucht, natürliche Verformungsmuster aus der Tierwelt auf einen Entwurf zu übertragen. Obwohl die Idee sehr verlok-

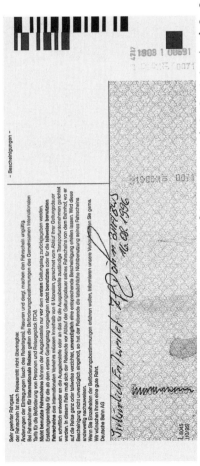

I say "idea" I don't always mean the same thing as Edi and Timmy do. The difference is probably that I tend to position the idea outside the direct function of a project. The thought of the bar code on the Coop façade or the Sierpinsky cube in the Breite do have something to do with the function of the building but they also exist without the building. They are somehow independent.

TON Which brings advantages and disadvantages in both directions. Certainly an abstract idea can give power to a project. But sometimes the idea develops too independently from the project itself. Then you have to look very carefully to see whether the idea can be implemented at all under the given circumstances. Only recently we tried, for example, to transfer natural distortion patterns from the animal world to a design. Although the idea was very enticing we had to abandon it because it did not fit in with the job we were doing at the time.

And another remark about questioning established images: when you see for a second or third time how images have changed because social structures have changed, then one becomes more distanced from the specific image. One starts to make a distinction between what effectively is change and what is just a fashionable phenomenon.

Searching for the one truth

CF Where are the fields in which you will be operating in the future?

TON I see a problem in the compulsive rush – already institutionalized – towards a complete lack of culture. The function of

Lehr-, Prüf- und Beratungszentrum, Basel,
Schweizerischer Verein für Schweiss-
technik, 1991-1994
**Teaching, Testing and Consultation
Centre, Basel, Swiss Welding
Technology Association, 1991-1994**

Das Grundstück liegt unmittelbar **The site is right at the head of a**
am Kopf einer Autobahnbrücke **motorway bridge over the Rhine**
über den Rhein und ist Bestand- **and is part of a development en-**
teil eines Überbauungsplanes, der **tailing a perimeter development**
eine Randbebauung um einen zen- **around a central garden court.**
tralen Gartenhof vorschreibt. **The site is very badly polluted**
Durch seine Lage neben der sechs- **on its eastern side by emissions**
spurigen Autobahn und einer Ei- **from the six-lane motorway and**
senbahnlinie ist das Grundstück **a railway line. The client's re-**
von Osten her stark immissions- **quest for quiet, naturally venti-**
belastet. Dem Wunsch der Bau- **lated rooms was met by a comp-**

kend war, mussten wir sie aufgeben, weil sie mit der Aufgabe nicht zur Deckung kam.
Und noch eine Bemerkung zur Infragestellung etablierter Bilder: Wenn man zum zweiten oder dritten Male erlebt, wie Bilder sich gewandelt haben, weil die Gesellschaftsstrukturen sich gewandelt haben, dann erhält man eine grössere Distanz zum spezifischen Bild. Man fängt an zu unterscheiden, was effektiv Wandel ist und was nur eine Modeerscheinung.

Die Suche nach der einen Wahrheit

CF Wo seht Ihr Eure Aufgabenbereiche in der Zukunft?

TON Ich sehe ein Problem im fast schon institutionalisierten Zwang zur Kulturlosigkeit. Die Funktion des Architekten wird die sein, zu den utilitaristischen Formulierungen eines Auftrags, die je länger je stärker auftreten, andere Werte in die Lösung einzubringen. Eigenartigerweise sträubt sich sehr oft der Auftraggeber dagegen.

CF Ist der Auftraggeber utilitaristisch oder hat er noch keine Bilder, an denen er sich orientieren kann?

TON Ich glaube, das zweite. Er spürt oft ein gewisses Bedürfnis nach Bildern, aber er weiss den Weg dorthin nicht.

CF Für mich ist es eindeutig das zweite. Unser Auftrag wäre, die Bilder zu formulieren.

TON Es ist die Aufgabe der Architekten, eine Brücke zwischen dem Utilitaristischen und dem Ideellen herzustellen. Das unterscheidet sie von den Maschinenbauern einerseits und den Künstlern andererseits. Diese Brückenfunktion müssen wir nicht nur für uns wahrnehmen, sondern auch für die Allgemeinheit.

CF Daniel, bist Du gleicher Mei-

architects will be to add furthe[r] values to solutions intended t[o] meet the utilitarian formula[tions] of a commission, whic[h] become stronger as time goe[s] on. Strangely enough clients ar[e] often resistant to this.

CF Are clients utilitarian, or i[s] it that they don't have image[s] to show them the way?

TON I think the latter. They of[ten] sense a need for images, bu[t] do not know how to find them.

CF For me it is unquestionabl[y] the latter. And it would be ou[r] job to formulate the images.

TON It is the architects' job t[o] build a bridge between the utili[tarian] and the ideal. This dis[tinguishes] them from mechani[cal] engineers on the one han[d] and artists on the other. An[d] we must not exercise this bridg[ing] function just for ourselve[s] but for everybody.

CF Daniel, do you agree?

DW Yes. In my view uncertaint[y] relating to current systems o[f] values is an important reaso[n] for the conservative attitude o[f] a lot of clients. Because an in[vestor] is not familiar with th[e] needs of the new tenant gener[ation] he goes back to tried and-tested ground plans eve[n] though people are rapidl[y] changing the way in which the[y] live. As money is getting tighte[r] at present this trend will prob[ably] be reinforced. It will b[e] very difficult to build a visio[n] in this context.

TON The client's loss of pe[r]sonality also has a part to pla[y] here. Formerly one or tw[o] people would be responsibl[e] over a long period, even in larg[e] firms. Today directions chang[e] much more rapidly. Companie[s] become more anonymous, an[d] so do the projects.

CF In my opinion the proble[m] today lies very much with th[e]

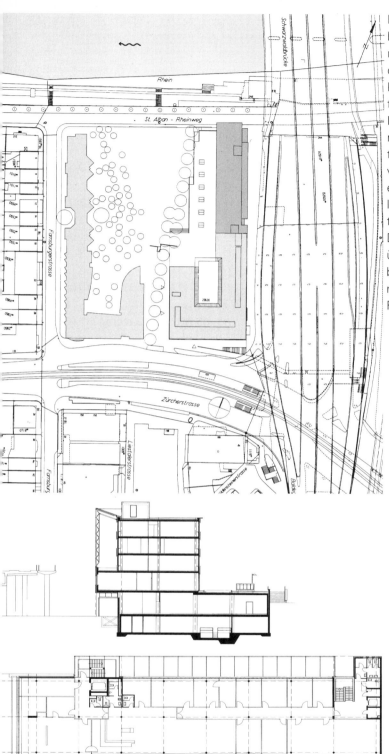

herrschaft nach ruhigen, natürlich **lex with three "naves". Two of** belüfteten Räumen wird mit ei- **these "naves" form a conven-** ner dreischiffigen Anlage entspro- **tional office building with cen-** chen. Zwei «Schiffe» bilden einen **tral corridor, and the third is con-** konventionellen Bürobau mit Zen- **ceived as noise garden forming** tralgang, das dritte «Schiff» ist als **a naturally ventilated buffer on** Lärmgarten konzipiert, der einen **the motorway side. Air flows in** natürlich belüfteten Puffer zur Au- **from the Rhine side and stale air** tobahn bildet. Die Zuluft fliesst **feeds out naturally though glass** von der Rheinseite her, die Abluft **slats in the roof of the noise** entweicht natürlich über Glas- **garden.** lamellen im Dach des Lärmgar- **The end on the Rhine side pro-** tens. **trudes over a public ramp con-** Der Kopf zum Rhein hin kragt **necting the level of the new** über eine öffentliche Rampenver- **Rhine bridge with the embank-** bindung aus, die vom Niveau der **ment.** neuen Rheinbrücke hinunter zum Rheinufer führt.

Situation 1:2000
Site plan 1:2000
Querschnitt 1:650
Section 1:650
Grundriss 3. Obergeschoss 1:650
3rd floor ground plan 1:650

41

nung?

DW Ja. In meinen Augen ist die Unsicherheit in Bezug auf gültige Wertsysteme ein wichtiger Grund für die konservative Haltung vieler Bauherren. Weil ein Investor den Bedarf der neuen Mietergenerationen nicht kennt, greift er auf bewährte Grundrisse zurück, obwohl die Wohnformen stark im Wandel sind. Da die finanziellen Mittel zur Zeit knapper werden, wird sich dieser Trend wohl noch verstärken. In diesem Kontext wird es sehr schwer sein, eine Vision zu bauen.

TON Auch der Persönlichkeitsverlust des Bauherrn spielt hier eine Rolle. Früher haben auch bei einer grossen Firma ein oder zwei Personen die Verantwortung langfristig übernommen. Heute werden die Direktionen viel schneller ausgewechselt. Es kommt zu einer Anonymisierung der Firmen und damit auch zu einer Anonymisierung der Projekte.

CF Nach meiner Meinung liegt das Problem heute sehr stark bei den Architekten: Sie müssten den Bauherren Bilder geben, die den heutigen Wertvorstellungen entsprechen. Muttenz und der Wettbewerb in der Breite sind für mich gute Beispiele dafür. Das sind Projekte, die insbesondere in Bezug auf die Bilder aktuell sind.

Spezifisch für unsere heutige Situation ist, dass das Produkt dieser Suche nicht eine allgemeine Wahrheit ist, sondern immer wieder eine neue Wahrheit.

TON In letzter Zeit ist oft die Rede von der neuen Einfachheit.

CF Ja, das ist zu einfach. Heute muss jeder von uns akzeptieren, dass er mit mehreren Wahrheiten konfrontiert ist und mit ihnen leben muss. Die Moderne mit Ihrer Lehre von der einen Wahrheit ist vorbei.

DW Es ist alarmierend, dass Ar-

architects: they have to arm cli[ents] with images that are compatible with today's moral concepts. I think that Muttenz and the Breite competition are good examples of this. These are projects that are particularly up to date in terms of images.

It is specific for our current situation that the product of this search is not just a general truth, but always a new truth.

TON There has been a lot of talk recently about a "new simplicity".

CF Yes, that is too simple. Today each of us has to accept that one is confronted with several truths and has to live with them. Modernism with its doctrine of one truth has gone.

DW It is alarming that architecture is nevertheless still discussed on the plane of style. An example of this is the most recent "firmitas" discussion at the ETH.

CF Yes, precisely because they are still looking for the correct solution. It seems to me that the ETH still tends to look for a new harmony, a new unity, a new style.

I was invited to Weimar to take part in a symposium arranged by the BDA (Federation of German Architects) town planning group, called 'In what style should we plan?'.

There is no answer to these questions today. A new solution has to be found each time.

DW Questions about style, correct use of materials and texture have developed into a discussion that is just for architects. While developments in society carry on unheeded the good architects wall themselves up in a fortress of structural truth and all the other old values of their discipline.

chitektur trotzdem auf der Ebene des Stils diskutiert wird. Ein Beispiel dafür ist die jüngste «firmitas»-Diskussion an der ETH.

CF Ja, weil sie eben immer noch nach der richtigen Lösung suchen. Es scheint mir, dass die ETH-Situation immer noch geprägt ist von der Suche nach einer neuen Harmonie, nach einer neuen Einheitlichkeit, nach einem neuen Stil.

Ich war eingeladen nach Weimar an ein Symposium von der Fachgruppe Stadtplanung der BDA (Bund Deutscher Architekten) mit dem Titel: ‹In welchem Stil sollen wir planen?›.

Auf diese Fragen gibt es heute keine Antwort. Man muss die Lösung eben jedesmal wieder neu finden.

DW Die Fragen des Stils, der Materialgerechtigkeit, der Textur haben sich zu einer reinen Architektendiskussion entwickelt. Während die Entwicklungen in der Gesellschaft unbeobachtet weiterlaufen, vermauern sich die guten Architekten hinter einer Festung von Konstruktionswahrheit und anderen alten Werten ihrer Disziplin.

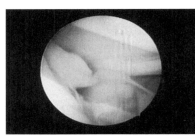

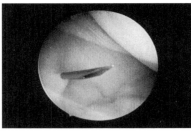

Das ist auch der Grund, wieso ich meinen Architekturvortrag in Basel mit dem Video meiner Knieoperation begonnen habe: Es ist doch seltsam, dass die starken und repräsentativen Bilder für unsere Zeit in anderen Fachbereichen entstehen. Sie scheinen vorhandene Kräfte und technische Entwicklungen viel unvoreingenommener zu nutzen.

CF Ärzte und Architekten sind für mich gegenwärtig die kulturell konservativsten Berufsgruppen. Die Bauherren sind eben manchmal weiter als die Architekten.

That is also the reason why I started my architecture lecture in Basel with a video of my knee operation: it is surely strange that the powerful and prestigious images of our days come from other fields. They seem to use existing forces and technical developments with a much more open mind.

CF For me doctors and architects are culturally the most conservative professional groups today. In fact the clients are often ahead of the architects.

Dreifach-Turnhalle Gundeldinger Schul-
haus, Basel, Baudepartement Basel-Stadt,
1991
**Triple Gymnasium, Gundeldinger
School, Basel, Basel-Stadt Building
Department, 1991**

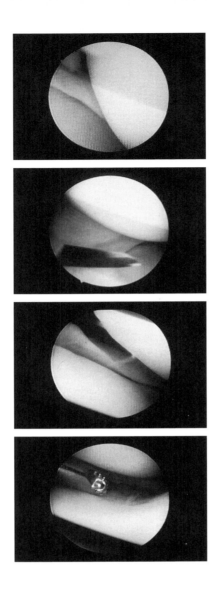

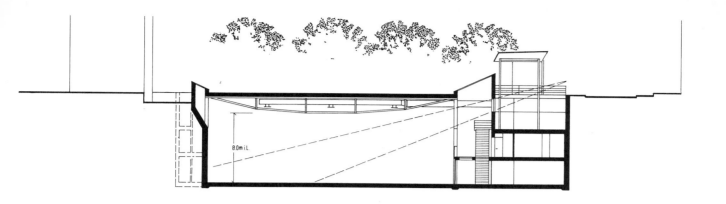

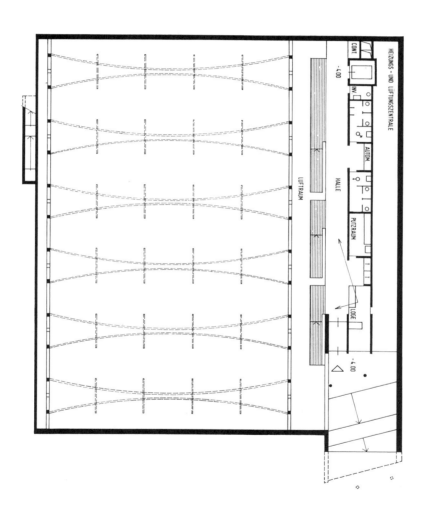

Schnitt 1:450
Section 1:450
Grundriss 1:450
Ground plan 1:450

Das Trojanische Pferd
Von der meist verlorenen Unschuld der Materialien
The Trojan Horse
About the Innocence – Largely Compromised – of Materials

Drei Systeme bilden einen Bau – die Materialien, das konstruktive System, das formale System – alle in sich schon vielfältig genug. Eingebunden in die funktionellen, sozialen, kulturellen, zeitlichen und ökonomischen Aufgaben und Rahmenbedingungen der Bauaufgabe entsteht eine unendliche Fülle an möglichen Lösungen.

Aber: Bauherr, Architekt, Öffentlichkeit, alle schränken ihren Handlungsspielraum ein, entwickeln – oder beachten zumindest – Paradigmen, Haltungen, die von sozialen, kulturellen, ökonomischen oder technischen Kräften geformt sind. Aus der Haltung der Zeit entwickeln sich Stile (aus den Stilen oft Schemata). Der Stil beeinflusst und formt die Zeit, ein Zwang – oder Zuneigung – zur Konformität wird spürbar, ist unumgänglich. Beispiele aus jüngerer Vergangenheit: Internationalismus, High-Tech, Regionalismus, neue Einfachheit.

Sich in diesem Gewebe unbelastet und unmittelbar zu verhalten, fällt schwer: Selten werden die verwendeten Konstruktionen und Konstruktionsmittel originär sein. Meist rekrutieren sie sich aus schon lange Erprobtem. Oft werden auch bereits schon bekannte formale Typologien angewendet.

Aus Materialien, spezifischen Kombinationen von konstruktiven Systemen entwickeln sich daher Bedeutungen, Symbole und Deutungen: Stein = repräsentativ, gesichert, dauerhaft; Holz = persönlich, unprätentiös, umweltbewusst (bis vor kurzem auch: provisorisch); Stahl = fortschrittlich, aktiv, technisch beherrscht; symmetrische Gestaltung lässt auf gesellschaftlich Bedeutendes schliessen; Alu-Gussformen markieren Fortschrittsglauben etc., etc.

Three systems make up a building – the materials, the construction system and the formal system – all quite complex enough in themselves. The process is inextricably linked with the functional, social, cultural, temporal and economic aspects surrounding any particular building job. This adds up to an infinite number of possible solutions.

But: client, architect, public, all restrict their scope for action work out – or at least pay attention to – paradigms, attitudes that are formed by social, cultural, economic or technical forces. Styles develop from the attitudes of the time (and platitudes often develop from the styles). Style influences and shapes time, a compulsion – or an inclination – to conformity can be sensed, becomes unavoidable. Examples from the recent past: internationalism, hightech, regionalism, new simplicity.

It is difficult to behave directly and in a carefree fashion in this web: the constructions and structural devices used will rarely be original. Usually they are recruited from tried and tested sources. Often formal typologies that are already familiar are used as well.

Meanings, symbols and interpretations develop from materials and specific combinations of structural systems: stone prestigious, secure, durable; timber = personal, unpretentious, environmentally aware (and until recently: temporary); steel progressive, active, technically controlled; symmetrical design suggests social significance; cast aluminium shows a belief in progress etc. etc.

Every material, every form, every construction system is occu

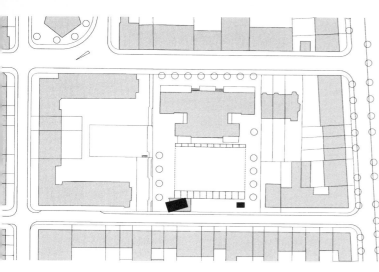

Im Bereich des Pausenplatzes einer Primar- und Sekundarschule muss eine Dreifach-Turnhalle erstellt werden. Die räumliche Enge verlangt nach einer unterirdischen Lösung, welche zudem in sehr kurzer Zeit erstellt werden muss, um die Nutzung der Pausenflächen nicht allzu lange zu blockieren.

Das Projekt verlegt konsequent alle Funktionen in die Untergeschosse. Sogar der Eingang wird an einen abgesenkten Hof angeschlossen, damit der Weg ins Untergeschoss bewusst erlebbar und auch für Passanten vom Trottoir aus einsehbar ist. Alle wesentlichen Funktionen werden über eine offene Galerie entlang der Turnhallen erschlossen. Durchgehende Oberlichter filtern hier Tageslicht mit seinen wechselnden Stimmungen in die Nebenräume und bis auf den 12 m tief gelegenen Turnhallenboden.

A triple gymnasium had to be built in the area occupied by the playground of a primary and secondary school. Lack of space called for an underground solution, and construction had to be completed very quickly so that the use of the playground area was disrupted as little as possible.

Thus, logically, all the functions were housed in the basement levels. Even the entrance has been linked to a sunken courtyard so that the way into this level can be enjoyed consciously, and can also be seen by passers-by on the pavement. Access to all the main functions is via an open gallery running along the gymnasia. Here continuous skylights filter daylight with its changing moods into the side rooms and right down to the gymnasium floors, which are 12 metres below ground level.

Situation 1:2500
Situation 1:2500

Jedes Material, jede Form, jedes Konstruktionssystem wird besetzt, mit Assoziationen und Deutungen belegt: Kein Material ist «unschuldig», kein konstruktives System «neutral». Allein schon der heute oft bemühte Begriff des «Paradigmenwechsels» unterstreicht, wie stark die Orientierung auf oder die Abhängigkeit von gesellschaftlich anerkannten Bedeutungen ist, sei es, um sie weiterführen, sei es, um sie – als Paradigma – auszuwechseln.

Diese gefestigten Bedeutungen vergehen aber auch wieder:

• Die Gesellschaft ändert sich und damit ihre Bilder, ihre Abbildungen: ein natürlicher und willkommener Prozess, auch wenn er sich oft umstürzlerisch vollzieht.

• Da die Form leichter zu erfassen ist als der Inhalt, kann es geschehen, dass die verwendeten Materialien oder konstruktiven Systeme zu leeren Formeln, zu Floskeln verkommen: das Mondfenster mag hier als unverfängliches Beispiel dienen. Form und Gehalt decken sich nicht mehr; es zeigen sich Widersprüche. Die Deutung, die «Belegung» ermüdet, es bleibt nur noch Hülle übrig. Dann wird ein Bau allenfalls in eine Assoziationswelt eingebunden, die nicht beabsichtigt war; oder er bleibt sogar assoziationslos, er wird unkenntlich in einem weiten Feld gleicher Formeln.

• Die Bilder, auch wenn sie eigentlich noch mit Inhalt angefüllt wären, werden übernutzt, sodass die damit verbundene Haltung an Gewicht verliert: die Symmetrie gilt noch immer als aussagekräftiges Gestaltungsmittel, sie wird aber oft als ausgelaugt empfunden.

• Die Bilder verlieren an Eindeutigkeit: die Bedeutung des Betons bei Toni Garniers «cité industri-

pied, overlaid with association and interpretations: no material is "innocent", no construction system "neutral". The concept of a "change of paradigm" which is often called upon today, alone underlines how strongly orientation towards or dependence on socially accepted meanings is, whether to take those meanings further or to change them – as paradigms.

But these fixed meanings also disappear again:

• Society changes itself, and thus changes its images, its illustrations: a natural and welcome process, even if it often happens subversively.

• As form is easier to grasp than content, it can happen that the materials or construction systems used degenerate into empty formulae, into clichés: the moon window can stand as a harmless example here. Form and content no longer coincide; contradictions start to show. The interpretation, the "occupation" peters out, only a husk is left. Then a building is at best tied into a world of associations that was not intended; or it even remains without associations, it becomes unrecognizable in a broad field of similar formulae.

• The images, even if they were still filled with content, are overused, so that the attitude associated with them loses its weight: symmetry is still considered to be an expressive design device, but it is often felt to be exhausted.

• Images lose their unambiguousness: the meaning of concrete in Tony Garnier's "cité industrielle" on the one hand and the slab construction building in post-war eastern Europe on the other will serve to support this.

As there is an interplay be

Freibad «Im Schlipf», Riehen, Gemeinde
Riehen, 1992
"Im Schlipf" Open-Air Swimming-Pool, Riehen, Riehen Municipality, 1992

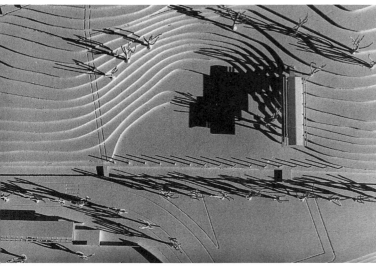

Das Planungsgebiet liegt einge-spannt zwischen dem Fluss «Wie-se» und dem wandernden Berg «Schlipf». Genaue «Langzeit-Kar-ten» dieses Berges erinnern an die Darstellung von Kometen: Je-der Punkt hat einen Schweif, der die Bewegung der letzten Jahre aufzeigt. Bis zu ihrer Begradigung hat die «Wiese» den Fuss des Ber-ges laufend abgetragen und so zu seinem Abrutschen beigetra-gen.

Die Projektierung des neuen Frei-bades war vor allem dadurch er-schwert, dass das Planungsgebiet

The planning area is between the river "Wiese" and the shift-ing "Schlipf" mountain. Precise "long-term maps" of this moun-tain are reminiscent of pictures of comets: each point has a tail showing its movement in the last few years. Until it was re-channelled the "Wiese" contin-ually eroded the foot of the mountain and thus made it slip all the more.

Designing the new swimming-pool was mainly hampered by the fact that the planning area was cut into three by a road, a

elle» einerseits und bei Platten-
bauten der Nachkriegszeit in Ost-
europa anderseits mögen dies
untermalen.

Da es zwischen eingesetzten Mit-
teln und beabsichtigter Aussage
zu Wechselwirkungen kommt,
entsteht somit auch das Potential zu «Verwechsel-Wirkungen».
Belegungen können umgekehr-
te Wirkungen auslösen; zudem
kann ein System oder Material
mit mehr als einer Deutung verbunden sein: die Assoziationen,
welche «Glas» auslöst, reichen
von der industriellen Ausstrah-
lung des Crystal Palace über die
entmaterialisierte Illusionswelt
der «Gläsernen Kette» bis hin
zum aktuellen Minimalismus.

Hinzukommt, dass Auslöser
und Ergebnis oft schwer auszu-
machen, voneinander zu tren-
nen oder auseinanderzuhalten
sind.

Mögliche Verunklärungen und
Veränderungen in der Wechsel-
wirkung Bild und Deutung sind
also mannigfach: Veränderungen
im gesellschaftlichen Umfeld, Verlust in der Beziehung zwischen
Bild und Deutung, Abnutzung
des Bildes, Verlust an Ein-Deut-
igkeit der Deutung.

Vor diesem Hintergrund ist klar,
wie komplex es wird, wenn bewusst mit dem Auseinanderklaf-
fen von Haltung und Form gearbeitet wird, wenn eine Aufgabe
dazu reizt, Materialien einzuset-
zen, deren Deutungen im Grunde genommen mit den funktionellen oder technischen Anforderungen der Aufgabe nicht kom-
patibel sind. Ein Museum für
zeitgenössische Kunst sähe sich
gerne eben «zeitgenössisch», beispielsweise in Stahl und Glas; für
die Ausstellung zeitgenössischer
Kunst sind meist andere Materialien jedoch geeigneter. So werden oft gequälte Begründungen
vorgebracht, um die an sich nicht

tween means used and intended statement, there is thus also
a potential for "mistaken interplay". "Occupation" can have an
opposite effect from that intended; also a system of material can be associated with more
than one meaning: the associations triggered by "glass" extend from the industrial aura
of the Crystal Palace via the de-
materialized world of illusion
of the "Gläserne Kette" movement down to current minima-
lism. An additional feature is
that trigger and result are often difficult to make out, to se-
parate from each other, or to
keep apart.

Possible blurring and changes
in the interplay of image and
interpretation thus occur for a
variety of reasons: changes in
the social environment, loss of
the relationship between image
and interpretation, the image
wearing out, loss of unambigu-
ous interpretation.

Against this background it is
clear how complex it is to work
deliberately with the gap between attitude and form, when
a problem suggests using material whose interpretation is fundamentally incompatible with
the functional or technical requirements of the particular
piece of work. A museum for
contemporary art would like to
see itself as "contemporary" in
steel and glass; but in fact most
other materials are more suit-
able for showing such work.
Thus tortured reasoning is often called upon to justify the
use of inappropriate materials
or structural and formal systems. The Trojan horse phenomenon occurs:
The Trojan horse claimed to be
something different (a present)
from what is was (a trick to
smuggle men into the city of

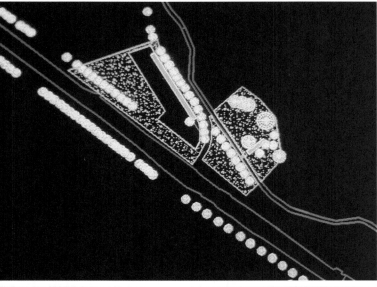

durch eine Strasse, einen Seiten-kanal der «Wiese» und einen unterirdischen Strassentunnel in drei Teile zerschnitten wird. Die Natur wird also bereits durch verschiedene kulturelle Eingriffe überlagert.

Das Projekt versucht, die einfachen Determinanten der Landschaft wieder herauszuschälen: Es fällt schwer, etwas Schöneres zu erfinden als einen wandernden Hügel.

Durch die Verlegung eines Fussweges, der normalerweise dem Fluss entlang führt, können die Flächen des neuen Schwimmbades zwischen Flussufer und Strasse untergebracht werden. So genügen die Flächen auf einer Seite der Strasse, um das Bad aufzunehmen. Die Strasse muss nicht überbrückt werden, der Fluss wird zur natürlichen Begrenzung des Bades, und am Fuss des Berges müssen keine Becken eingegraben werden.

Den zwei dominanten Elementen der Landschaft entsprechend sind zwei Baukörper vorgesehen: ein langer Garderobentrakt parallel zum Fluss und ein Gebäude senkrecht zum Fuss des Berges. Dieses ist nur über zwei Stützen fundiert, welche bis auf die tragfähige Steinschicht geführt sind, während der Hang darüber hinweg rutscht. Die eigenartige Gestalt dieses Gebäudes soll das Phänomen des «wandernden Hügels» lesbar machen.

Durch die räumliche Konzentration der Schwimmbecken und Garderoben kann ein Grossteil des Geländes im Herbst, Frühling und Winter der Öffentlichkeit freigegeben werden.

side canal leading into the "Wiese" and an underground road tunnel. Thus nature had already been overlaid by three different cultural interventions.

The project tried to put the emphasis back on the simple determinants of the landscape: it is difficult to invent something more beautiful than a hill with a landslip.

A footpath that used to run along the bank of the river was diverted to make it possible to place the new swimming-pool between the river-bank and the road, which meant that there was room for all the required facilities on one side of the road. There was no need for a bridge over the road, the river becomes a natural border for the swimming-pool and nothing had to be excavated at the foot of the mountain.

Two buildings are proposed, corresponding with the two dominant elements of the landscape: a long changing-room wing parallel with the river and a building set vertically to the slope near the foot of the mountain. This is supported by two columns only, which go right down to the load-bearing stratum of stone (over which the slope is sliding). The strange shape of this building is intended to make the phenomenon of the "sliding hill" intelligible.

Because the space devoted to the swimming-pool and changing-rooms is so compact in spatial terms it is possible to leave a large part of the site open to the public in autumn, spring and winter.

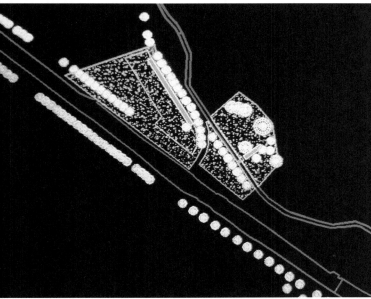

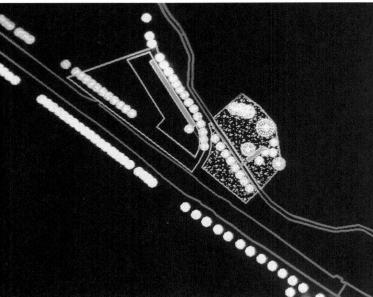

Nutzung in Wintertagen
Winter day (use)
Nutzung an Sommertagen
Summer day (use)
Nutzung in Sommernächten
Summer night (use)

stimmigen Materialien, konstruktiven oder formalen Systeme trotzdem einsetzen zu können. Es entsteht das Phänomen des trojanischen Pferdes:

Das trojanische Pferd gab an, etwas anderes zu sein (ein Geschenk) als es war (eine List, um Eingang in die Stadt Troja zu erhalten), weil die berechtigte Vermutung bestand, es würde in seiner wahren Aussage nicht akzeptiert. Die Griechen haben seinem Äusseren eine Erscheinung gegeben, die seiner Funktion nicht entsprach. Eine ähnliche Zweideutigkeit kann bei der Projektentwicklung Raum greifen. Wohnsiedlungen in der Form von Palastanlagen sind vielleicht nur ein extremer Ausdruck dieser «List».

Im Hinblick auf die Fährnisse, welche im Umgang mit belegten Elementen anstehen, ist die Lust, den Weg in die unbelastete Welt nicht belegter Materialien, zu wählen zwar verständlich, aber kaum wirklich möglich.

In der Auflehnung gegen gefestigte Belegungen können allenfalls neue Bilder entstehen, – oder alte werden mit neuen Deutungen belegt. Vielleicht entstehen auch neue spezifische formale Systeme, ein Material gewinnt neue Bedeutungen, – oder gewinnt neu an Bedeutung, aber selten in ursprünglicher Art, sondern eher als Umpolung schon bestehender Belegungen. Nicht nur für den Architekten bleibt diese Konfrontation vermutlich unumgänglich.

Troy) because there was a justifiable assumption that it would not be accepted in terms of its true statement. The Greeks gave it an outward appearance that was not appropriate to its function. Similar ambiguity can occur in project development. Housing estates in the form of palaces are perhaps just an extreme expression of this "trick." In view of the perils that lurk in the handling of occupied elements, the pleasure taken in venturing along the pathway of the unburdened world of unoccupied materials is understandable, but scarcely really possible.

New images can be created when resisting occupied systems – or old ones provided with new interpretations. Perhaps new specific formal systems will also come into being, a material acquires new meanings – or acquires meaning again, but seldom in the original way, but by reversing the polarity of existing occupations. This confrontation is presumably inevitable not only for architects.

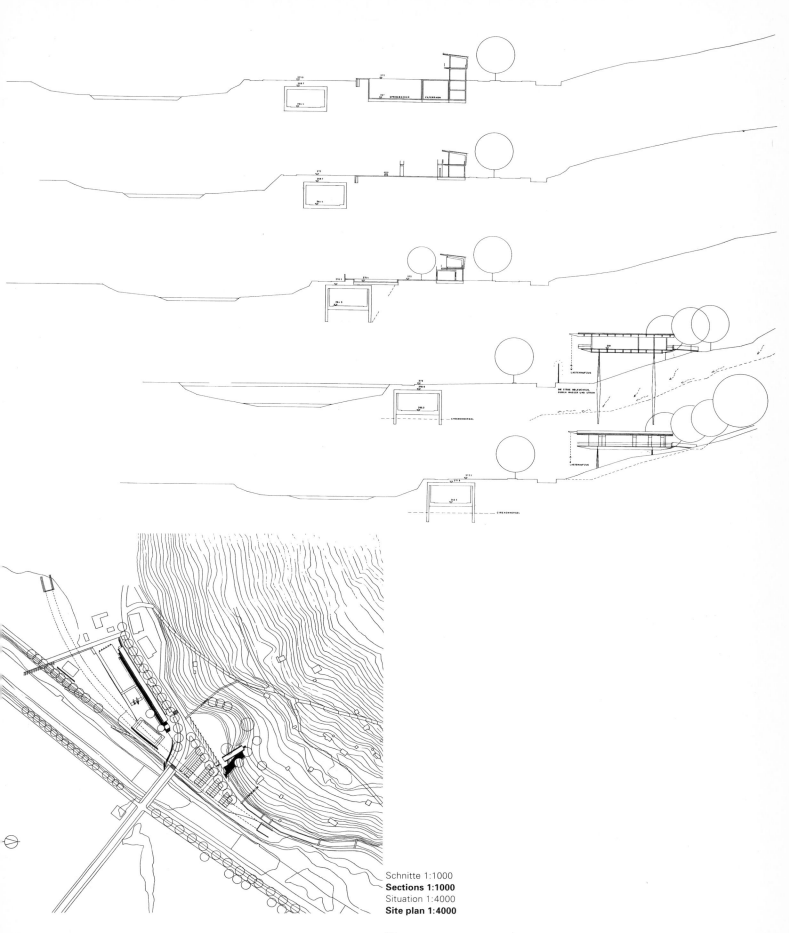

Schnitte 1:1000
Sections 1:1000
Situation 1:4000
Site plan 1:4000

57

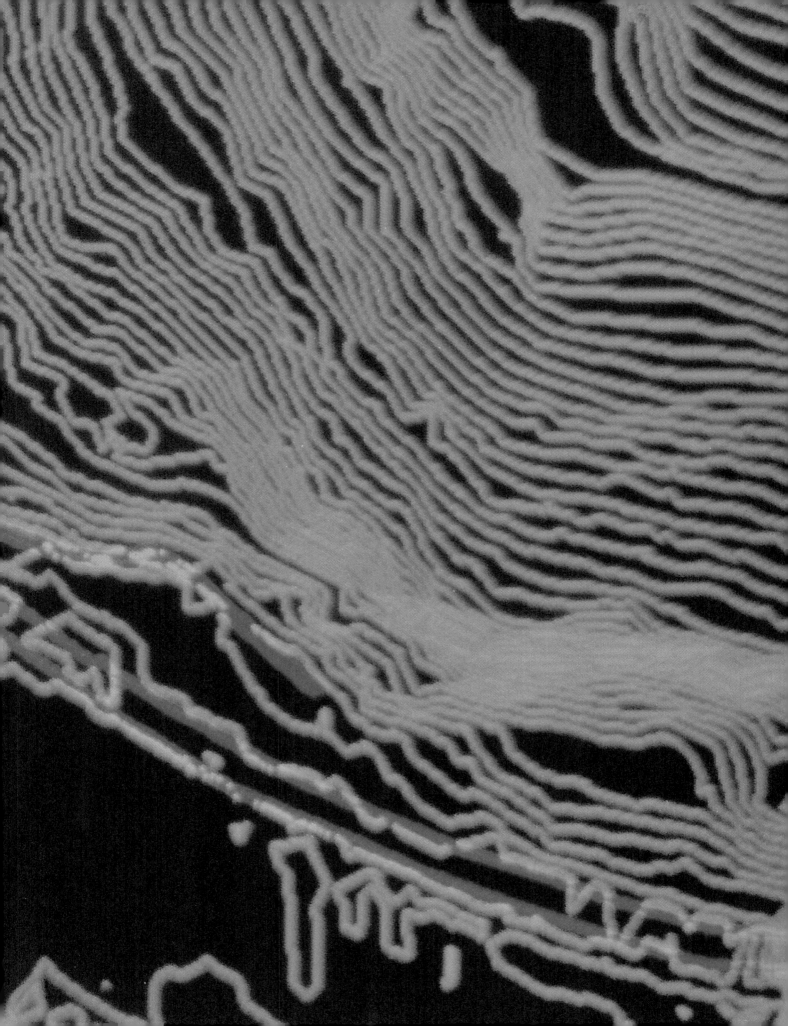

Schule für Gestaltung, Quartierzentrum
und Postfiliale, Basel, Baudepartement
Basel-Stadt, 1993
**School of Design, Neighbourhood
Centre and Post Office, Basel,
Basel-Stadt Building Department, 1993**

Randerscheinungen
Peripheral Phenomena, or the Essence of Edges

Ohne Rand entsteht eine Welt ohne Grenzen. Der Rand lässt das Umfeld greifbar werden, massstäblich. Durch amorphe Zonen gezogen, kann der Rand klärend, ordnend wirken. Nur wenn Dinge einen Rand haben, sind sie ein «Ding», werden also für unser Bewusstsein vorstellbar. Das Weltall hat keinen Rand. Luft hat unendlich viele Ränder, weil sie immer dort aufhört, wo sie ein Objekt umhüllt.

Oder: Am Rand verdichtet sich der Inhalt. Er wirkt wie eine Zusammenfassung seines Hinterlandes. Die wesentlichen Züge des vom Rande Umfassten bilden sich am Rande ab. Er wirkt wie eine Netzhaut, auf der sich die Aussenwelt abbildet, wie eine Schnittfläche durch ein anatomisches Präparat und macht den Inhalt erkennbar und lesbar. Der Rand kann Abbildung, «Fangfläche» der Eigenschaften oder Struktur eines Inhaltes sein. Und so, wie er Inhalte abzeichnet, kann er auch – zeitlich verstanden – Ereignisse abzeichnen. Denn der Rand kann Räumliches, Zeitliches, aber auch Begriffliches begrenzen (am Rande der Stadt, am Rande der Gegenwart, am Rande des Bewusstseins).

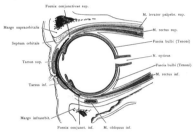

Oder: Der Rand ist nur Trennung von Gleichartigem, wie ein Zaun oder eine Mauer oder ein Fluss. Oder: Der Rand ist eine Hülle, die das Innere kaum oder gar nicht zu erkennen gibt wie die Orangenschale. Wie der Rand eingrenzt, so kann er auch ausgrenzen, Schutzhülle sein, Pufferzone bilden, aber auch «Randständiges» kreieren.

Oder: Der Rand ist eine Membrane, zu deren Durchdringung besondere Fähigkeiten und Eigenschaften erforderlich sind. Die Durchquerung wird zum Ereignis. Sie kann physisch erfolgen, sie kann im Bewusstsein oder

If there is no periphery, no edge we are faced with a world without boundaries. An edge make the environment comprehensible, gives it a scale. An edge running through amorphous zones can be explanatory and impose order. A thing only becomes a "thing" when it has an edge, and so becomes open to our awareness. The universe has no periphery. Air has an infinity of peripheries, because it always stops where it surrounds an object.

Or: content becomes denser on the periphery. It seems like a summary of its hinterland. The essential features of what an edge contains are illustrated on that edge. It works like a retina on which the outside world is depicted, like a section through an anatomical specimen, making the contents recognizable and intelligible. The edge can be an illustration, a "catcher-surface" for qualities or the structure of a content. And as it delineates content it can also – in terms of time – delineate events For an edge, a verge, can limit space (at the edge of the town and time (on the verge of the present), but also concepts (on the periphery of consciousness Or: an edge is just something that separates like from like – a fence or a wall or a river.

Or: an edge is a cover that totally or partially conceals what is inside, like an orange peel Just as an edge includes, it can exclude, be a protective covering, a buffer zone, but also create "marginal" conditions.

Or: the edge is a membrane needing particular abilities and qualities if it is to be penetrated Crossing it becomes an event. I can be physical, or simply a conscious event or something visua Crossing an edge is crossing

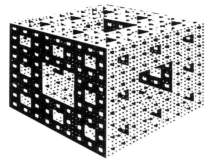

Alle drei Funktionen des Programmes, die Schule für Gestaltung, das Quartierzentrum und die Postfiliale, sind öffentlichkeitsorientiert. Die Hauptaufgabe des Projektes besteht in der nachvollziehbaren Einbindung dieser Funktionen in das städtische Raumgefüge.

Das Breiteareal liegt an der Kreuzung zweier Verkehrswege mit gegensätzlichem Charakter: Während der Rhein Ruhe und Gleichmässigkeit ausstrahlt, belastet die Autobahn ihre Umgebung mit Lärm, hartem Licht und schnellen Bewegungen. Die Autobahn verlangt nach Abgrenzung, der Rhein verdient Zuwendung und Öffnung. Dieses Spannungsfeld zwischen Geschlossenheit und Öffnung, Abwendung und Zuwendung führt zum Bild eines Schwammes: nach aussen hin ein kompaktes, monolithisches Gebilde, im Inneren jedoch eine komplex verwobene Landschaft aus Höhlen und Gängen. Über diese Hohlräume geht das Gebäude eine Beziehung zu seiner Umgebung ein.

All three of this project's functions, the design school, the neighbourhood centre and the post-office are aimed at the public. The main task was to integrate these functions into the urban structure in an intelligible fashion.

The Breite site is at the junction of two transport routes that are entirely different in character: while the Rhine radiates calm and regularity, the motorway pollutes its environment with noise, hard light and rapid movement. The motorway needs to be shielded, and the Rhine deserves to be opened up and to have attention drawn to it. This field of tension between being open and closed, turning to and turning away, leads to the image of a sponge: to the outside it is a compact, monolithic structure, but inside a complex, interwoven landscape of hollows and passages. The building enters into a relationship with its surroundings via these cavities.

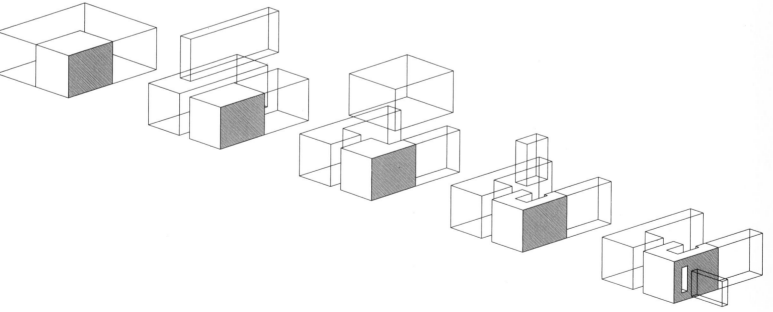

Sierpinskys Würfel
Sierpinsky cube
Räumliches Konzept
Spatial concept

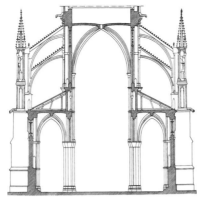

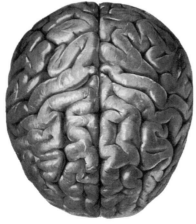

nur visuell erfolgen. Der Gang über einen Rand ist ein Gang über eine Schwelle, gleichgültig, ob sich die Eigenschaften diesseits und jenseits ändern oder nicht.

Bei einzelnen Rändern liegt ihr Wert in ihrem möglichst kurzen Verlauf (z.B. Stadtmauer), bei anderen in der möglichst grossen Ausdehnung und damit in einer grossen Kontaktfläche mit dem Umfeld (z.B. Verzahnung von Stadt und Grün).

Oder: Ränder «benehmen» sich auch im Hinblick auf verschiedene Eigenschaften verschieden. Was für die räumliche Bewegung eine Barriere bedeutet, kann visuell durchlässig sein. Was im Stadträumlichen ein Zeitrand sein kann (beispielsweise zwischen Altstadt und City), kann funktionell homogen sein (beispielsweise Einkaufszone), also: ambivalente oder gar polyvalente Ränder bilden.

Der Rand kann auch geschichtet ausgebildet sein, so dass er seinen Inhalt nur zaghaft, dosiert, nach Anstrengungen preisgibt.

Die Genauigkeit des Randes ist eine Frage der Betrachtungsweise: ob vom Weltall aus, vom Flugzeug, vom Auto, zu Fuss, mit dem Mikroskop. Wir haben es als Architekten oft in der Hand, die Perspektive zu wählen, zu bestimmen.

Schliesslich können Ränder ihre Eigenschaften ändern, sich verdichten, sich auflösen, anfänglich abweisend, dann empfangend wirken.

Je bewusster der Umgang mit den Rändern in ihren vielfältigen Ausprägungen, desto stärker wird ein wertvolles Gestaltungspotential genutzt.

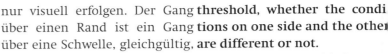

threshold, whether the conditions on one side and the other are different or not.

Some edges are valuable because they are as short as possible (e.g. a city wall), others need to be as long as possible and touch their surroundings as much as possible (e.g. the points where the city meets the green belt). Or: edges "behave" differently in terms of various qualities. Something that acts as a barrier to movement can be transparent to the eye. Something that has an edge in terms of time (for example the line between the old and the new town) can be functionally homogeneous (a shopping district, for example) in other words there can be ambivalent or polyvalent edges.

An edge can also be structured in layers, so that it reveals its content only by degrees, in doses, after an effort.

The precise quality of an edge is determined by the way we look at it: from space, from an aircraft, from a car, on foot through a microscope. We as architects often have the power to choose and to determine the viewpoint.

Finally, edges can change their qualities, condense, dissolve, first seeming daunting, but then welcoming.

The more consciously edges are handled in their various manifestations, the more powerfully a valuable element of design potential can be realized.

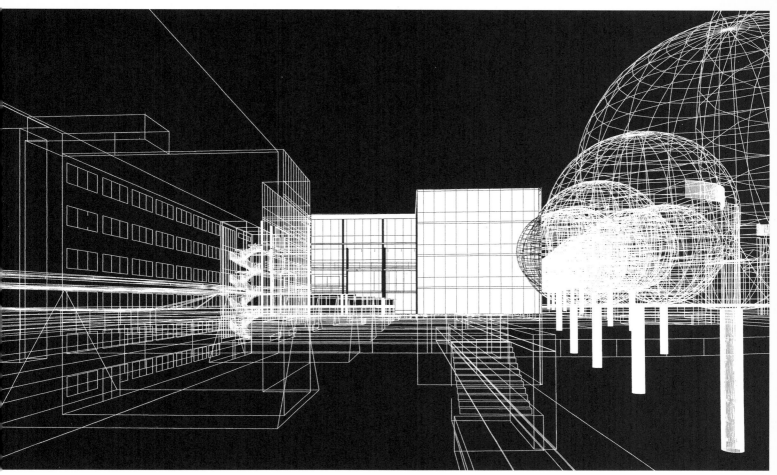

Aus einem regelmässigen Quader werden die öffentlichen Räume herausgeschnitten. Durch Überschneidungen sind sie zu einer zusammenhängenden, hierarchisch gegliederten Raumkaskade verwoben, die mit dem Rhein, dem wichtigsten öffentlichen Raum Basels, beginnt, über den gemeinsamen Innenhof des Blokkes zum privateren Innenhof von Quartierzentrum und Schule, dann in die Eingangshalle und schliesslich über die Cafeteria in die Aula führt.

Alle diese Räume sind funktionell und optisch miteinander verwoben. Die Räume verzahnen sich in einer Reihe von «transparenten» Überlagerungen.

The public spaces are cut out of a regular square. They overlap to form a coherent, hierarchically structured cascade of space, starting with the Rhine, Basel's most important public space, passing through the joint inner courtyard of the block to the more private inner courtyard of the neighbourhood centre and the school, then into the entrance hall and finally via the cafeteria into the hall.

All these spaces are linked functionally and visually. They are interconnected in a series of "transparent" overlapping features.

Perspektive vom Innenhof aus
Perspective view from the inner courtyard
Räumliches Konzept
Spatial concept

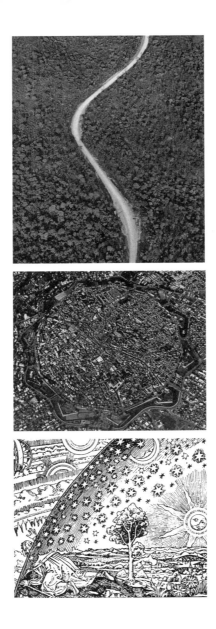

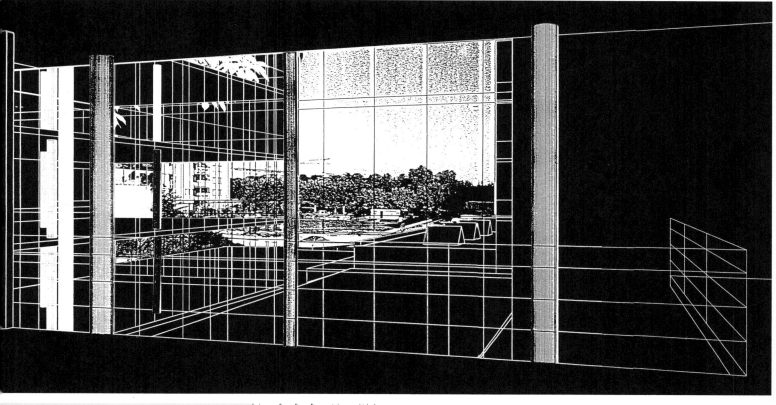

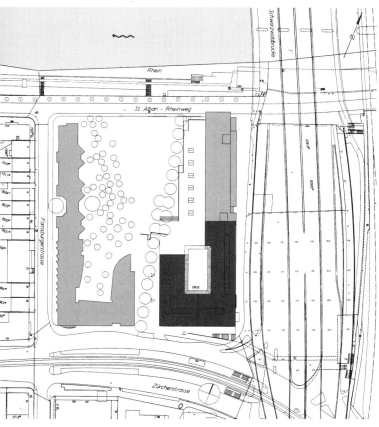

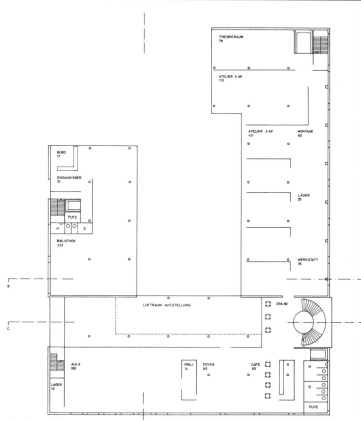

Blick in den Innenhof
View of courtyard
Situation 1:2000
Site plan 1:2000
Grundriss 1. Obergeschoss 1:550
First floor ground plan 1:550

Haus Burckhardt-Vischer, Umbau und
Erweiterung einer Remise zum Wohnhaus,
Rittergasse, Basel, 1992-1994
**Burckhardt-Vischer House, Coach-House
Conversion and Extension, Basel,
1992-1994**

Sinn-volles
Sens-ible

Der gewaltige Einfluss, den die Verdichtung und Vermengung von Zeit und Raum am Ende des letzten, anfang dieses Jahrhunderts durch die technologische (Telegraf, Telefon, Radio) und wissenschaftliche (Relativitätstheorie) Entwicklung genommen hat, dieses Phänomen, das sich beispielsweise im Futurismus manifestiert hat, hat zu einer Verschiebung in der Bedeutung der Sinne beigetragen: Die Gestaltungskultur der westlichen Welt ist noch sicht-lastiger geworden; eine latente Einseitigkeit der Wertung unserer Sinne wurde verstärkt. Die Sprache ist seit jeher sicht-lastig. Sie verwendet für abstrakte Begriffe zwar nicht ausschliesslich, aber sehr gerne seh-orientierte Ausdrücke (Absicht, Vorsicht, Vorsehung, Klarsicht, Umsicht, Zuversicht etc. etc.). Auch dieses Buch beschränkt sich weitgehend auf visuelle Übermittlung, kaum auf Vermittlung über das Gefühl (ausser dem Gewicht des Buches und der Beschaffenheit der Papieroberfläche). Ein erblickter Raum, ein gesehenes Stadtviertel oder Gebäude gelten für manchen schon als erlebt. Wenn das Sehen, unser bedeutendster Sinn, angesprochen und befriedigt worden ist, was will man mehr. Eine solche Einseitigkeit der Empfindung führt logischerweise auch zu Gestaltungskonzeptionen ähnlicher Gewichtung.

Nun ist dieser Seh-Sinn aber abstrakt, intellektuell, d.h. der unsinnlichste der Sinne. Wenn nur er allein angesprochen wird, so entsteht Unvollständiges, das Potential der Gestaltung bleibt brach, das Ergebnis leidet an Dürre, an Unerfülltheit. Denn die Sinne ergänzen sich, unterstützen sich, formen Erlebnisse und Reize der einzelnen Sinne zu einem Ganzen: «Die Probleme ent-

The enormous influence exercised by the intensification and mingling of time and space at the end of the last and the beginning of this century by technological developments (the telegraph, telephone, radio) and scientific developments (the theory of relativity), a phenomenon that came to the surface in Futurism, for example, has led to a shift in the significance of the senses: Western design culture had become more weighted towards sight; an already latent one-sidedness in our sensual evaluation was reinforced. The German language has been sight-weighted from time immemorial. It does not use expressions that are linked with sight to the exclusion of all others, but it is certainly very fond of them: the German word for sight is Sicht, then we have Absicht (intention), Vorsicht (foresight), Vorsehung (fore-seeing, providence; Sehung from sehen, to see), Klarsicht (transparency), Umsicht (circumspection), Zuversicht (confidence) etc. This book also confines itself largely to visual communication, rather than conveying ideas by feelings (except for the weight of the book and the surface qualities of the paper). Once a space has been sighted, a part of a town or a building seen, many people consider it to have been experienced. When sight, our most important sense, has been addressed and satisfied, what more can one want. Such one-sidedness in perception logically also leads to design concepts with a similar weighting. But this sense of sight is abstract and intellectual, i.e. the most unsensual of the senses. If it is the only sense to be addressed then what is produced i

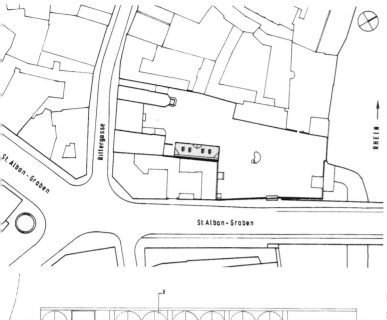

Eine Kutschen-Remise mit Stallungen aus dem 18. Jahrhundert soll zu einem Wohnhaus für ein Ehepaar um- und ausgebaut werden. Das Gebäude liegt in einer denkmalgeschützten Zone. Die Fläche der bestehenden Remise ist zu klein, um das Raumprogramm aufzunehmen; ihre Lage und Orientierung ergeben nur eine ungenügende Belichtung. Wie viele Ökonomiegebäude aus dieser Zeit ist sie als demontable Holzkonstruktion konzipiert.

Ein schmaler Lichtschlitz zwischen Bau und Rückwand und die «mobile» Konstruktionsart führen zur Idee der gläsernen Lücke: Der

An 18th century coach-house with stabling was to be converted and extended as a house for a married couple. The building is in a listed area. The area of the existing coach-house is too small to provide all the accommodation required, and its position and orientation make it very dark. Like many outbuildings of its period it was designed as a wooden structure that can be dismantled.

A narrow light-slit between the building and the back wall and the "mobile" nature of the structure suggested the idea of a glazed gap: the existing build-

Situation 1:1800
Site plan 1:1800
Grundriss Erdgeschoss 1:250
Ground floor plan 1:250
Grundriss 1. Obergeschoss 1:250
1st floor ground plan 1:250
Schnitt 1:250
Section 1:250

71

stehen durch die Isolation des Auges von seiner natürlichen Zusammenarbeit mit anderen Sinnesvorgängen und durch den Ausschluss und die Unterdrückung der anderen Sinne, was gesamthaft bewirkt hat, dass die Welt auf die Sphäre des Sehens reduziert und eingeschränkt wird.» (J. Pallasmaa, The Skin of the Eyes).
Manchmal verkümmern die Sinnbedürfnisse so weit, dass sie sich bei der Erfassung von Bauten und Räumen sogar mit dem Seh-Sinn allein begnügen: Der Anblick genügt, um Architektur empfunden zu haben, eine physische Begegnung ist nicht erforderlich, allenfalls sogar belastend oder verwirrend. Im Extremen gilt sogar die Abbildung als Erlebnis, als Empfindung, ohne die Belastungen der Wirklichkeit miterleben zu müssen.
Diese «Hegemonie der Sicht», wie sie Pallasmaa nennt, schafft Verlust an Empfindungsstärke, bringt Lust-Verlust. Eine bauliche Leistung, die allein auf diesen einen Sinn abstellt, ist arm.
Die bewusste Nutzung möglichst vieler Sinne gibt dem Raum grössere Kraft und grösseren Wert.
Wenn wir uns nur auf die klassischen Sinne, «Sehen», «Hören», «Fühlen», «Riechen» und «Schmecken» beschränken (und weitere «Sinne» wie den Zeitsinn, den Gleichgewichtssinn ausklammern), so sprechen wir mit Bauten vier bis fünf Sinne an. Eine bewusste Ausrichtung auf alle Sinne ist ungewohnt, aber bereichernd.
Die fünf Sinne besitzen unterschiedliche «Empfindungsnähen», unterschiedliche Fähigkeiten, Erinnerungen auszulösen (Gerüche sind besonders stark erinnerungsauslösend), und sie sind sehr unterschiedlich beschreibbar (visuelle Reize lassen sich für Dritte viel nachvollziehbarer beschrei-

incomplete, the design's poten tial lies fallow, and the resul becomes arid and unfulfilled The reason for this is that the senses complement each other support each other, shape experiences and stimuli from the individual senses into a whole "Problems are created by isolating the eye from its natural cooperation with other sensual processes, and by excluding and suppressing the other senses which has had the overall effect that the world is reduced and restricted to the sphere of seeing." (J. Pallasmaa, The Skin of the Eyes).
Sometimes the needs of the senses atrophy to the extent that they are content with the sense of sight when taking in buildings and rooms: a look is enough to have gained a sense of a piece of architecture, a physical confrontation is not required, or at best it is stressful or confusing. In extreme cases even an illustration counts as an experience, without having to cope with the strains of reality.
The "hegemony of sight" as Pallasmaa calls it, causes a loss of powerful sensation, a loss of pleasure. A building geared to this one sense is a poor one.
Conscious use of as many senses as possible gives a space greater power and greater value.
If we restrict ourselves only to the classical senses, "seeing", "hearing", "feeling", "smelling" and "tasting" (and exclude other "senses" like the sense of time or the sense of balance), then we are addressing buildings with four to five senses. A conscious approach to all the senses is at best unusual, but enriching.
The five senses have different "sensation thresholds", different abilities to trigger memo

bestehende Bau wird von der Gartenmauer abgerückt. So kann Zenitlicht grosszügig eindringen, während das Dach der alten Remise unverändert bleibt. Die neuen technischen Elemente des Wohnens wie Küche, Bad und Treppe werden frei hineingestellt, ohne die vorhandene Bausubstanz zu verletzen.

Der Glaskörper schafft eigentümliche Erscheinungen: Aus dem Bett geht der Blick nachts direkt hinauf in den Sternenhimmel, morgens bisweilen in Gewitterwolken. Dank der Öffnung des Erdgeschosses zum Garten und des Obergeschosses über den Glaskörper zum Himmel hin mischen sich im durchgehenden zweigeschossigen Raum aus dem Garten reflektiertes, leicht grün getöntes Licht mit weissem Zenitlicht.

ing is shifted away from the garden wall. Thus zenith light can flood in, while the old coachhouse roof remaines unchanged. The new technical elements of a house such as kitchen, bathroom and staircase will be on an open plan, without damaging the existing building.

The introduced glass element creates some strange phenomena: there is a direct view of the starry sky from bed at night, and in the mornings you can sometimes see thunderclouds. Thanks to the fact that the ground floor opens on to the garden and the upper floor to the sky through the glass roof, there is in the two-storey room that runs right through the building a mixture of slightly green light reflected from the garden and white zenith light.

ben und damit auch planen als Gerüche).

Eine Bewegung kann suggeriert werden, wenn durch die Wahl der gereizten Sinne bewusst verschiedene Empfindungsnähen angesprochen werden.

Zielt man stark auf die Geruchsempfindung ab, so werden für jeden einzelnen spezifische, anderen kaum vermittelbare und oft besonders trächtige Erinnerungen geschaffen.

Zum Gesicht:

Ein Bau wirkt von weitem schon auf den Seh-Sinn, und zwar räumlich, aber auch zeitlich: Kein anderer Sinn wird ausserdem so intensiv eingesetzt, Bauten vor ihrer eigentlichen Realisierung darzustellen. Räumliche Gefüge lassen sich am besten bildlich darstellen. Bild und Plan sind die üblichsten und prägendsten Medien der Architekturdarstellung. Sogar Modelle werden meist zur visuellen Darstellung verwendet, selten zur Vorstellung der haptischen Eigenschaften eines Baues, geschweige denn seiner Gefühlseigenschaften wie Temperatur oder Luftbewegung. Pläne, Modelle sind Vor-Bilder für die Wirklichkeit. Der Bau wird eben vorgebildet, nicht vorgehört oder vorgefühlt (wie in Huxleys «feelies»).

Zum Gehör:

Das akustische Erleben eines Gebäudes setzt erst später ein: die Qualität der Schallreflexion, bestimmt durch die Gebäudeform, dessen Oberflächen, aber auch durch die Nutzung des Gebäudes wie seines Umfelds prägen die Empfindung des Baues mit. Dieser Sinn wird aber eben erst in der Nähe wirksam, teilweise erst dann, wenn man den Bau betreten hat.

ries (smells are particularly strong memory triggers) and they are open to description in very different ways (visual stimuli are easier to describe to third parties, and thus to plan than smells).

A movement can be suggested i various sensation thresholds are consciously addressed by the choice of stimulated senses.

If the sense of smell is heavily involved, then very specific memories will be created for each individual; they are difficult to convey to others and often especially potent.

Sight:

A building affects the sense of sight even from a distance, in terms of both space and time No other sense is used so intensively to present buildings before they are actually realized Spatial structures are best presented as images. Picture and plan are the most usual and succinct ways of presenting architecture. Even models are mostly used for visual presentation, rarely as a way of evoking the tactile qualities of a building, to say nothing of felt qualities like temperature or the movement of air. Plans and models are images that precede reality. The building is presented in advance as an image, not as something heard or felt (as in Huxley's "feelies").

Hearing:

Acoustic appreciation of a building starts later: the quality of sound reflection, determined by the shape of the building, its surfaces but also the use of the building and its surroundings help to shape the way in which it is apprehended. But this sense is effective only from close by or on entering.

Niederlassung Birsfelden, Baselland-
schaftliche Kantonalbank, 1993-1996
Ladenpavillon, Peter Leuenberger,
1993-1996
**Birsfelden Branch, Basellandschaftliche
Kantonalbank, 1993-1996
Shopping Pavilion, Peter Leuenberger,
1993-1996**

Zum Geruch:

Der Geruch ist selten als Gestaltungsmittel bewusst «angesprochen», obwohl unbewusst die Wirkung eines Baues durch Gerüche mitbestimmt wird. Durch die Wahl der Materialien (Linolgeruch, der Geruch gewisser Holzarten, der Geruch von Stahl oder Aluminium, von einer neuen Maschine etc.), verbunden mit der Verteilung der Nutzungen im Gebäude (die Gerüche eines Kopierraumes, einer Garage, eines nahen Gewässers, eines selten verwendeten Treppenhauses sind oft unverwechselbar) sowie mit der Art und Führung der Lüftung (viel Frischluft kann einem Bau den spezifischen Geruch nehmen).

Zum Gefühl:

Das Gefühl (wie der Geschmack) können erst am Bau selber aktiviert werden, erst wenn ein physischer Kontakt entsteht. Beim Gefühl sind viele Facetten angesprochen: die Strukturen und Texturen einer räumlichen Begrenzung, die Temperaturen der Oberflächen, die Einwirkung verschiedener Strahlungen und Abstrahlungen, die Luftbewegungen, die Frequenz und Stärke der Bewegungen (Drehtüren, Lifte, Türen etc.), das Gefühl des veränderten Gleichgewichts auf geneigten Ebenen.

Zum Geschmack:

Der Geschmack wird selten explizit als Gestaltungssinn bei Bauten angesprochen. Dabei gibt es Bauten, bei denen just die Gestaltung des Geschmackes bei der architektonischen Gesamtlösung auschlaggebend oder zumindest bedeutungsvoll war. Zwei Beispiele zur Untermalung:
Die Villa Lante in Bagnaia (Abbildung), nahe bei Rom, auch nahe bei Caprarola, wo Vignolas

Smell:

Smell is rarely consciously "addressed" as a design device, although the impression made by a building is unconsciously determined by smell among other things. By the choice of certain materials (the smell of linoleum, of certain kinds of wood, of steel or aluminium, of a new machine etc.), the distribution of functions in a building (the smell of a photocopying room, a garage, a nearby waterway or even a rarely used staircase are unmistakable), the nature and direction of ventilation (a lot of fresh air can take away a building's specific smell).

Feeling:

Feeling (like taste) can only be activated by the building itself when there is actual physical contact. Many facets are addressed by feeling: the structures and textures of something that forms a boundary to a space, the temperature of surfaces, the effect of different kinds of radiation and reflection, the movement of air, the frequency and intensity of movements (revolving doors, lifts, doors etc.), a different feeling of balance on slopes.

Taste:

Taste is rarely addressed as a design sense in buildings. But there are buildings in which the design of taste is crucial or at least significant for the overall architectural solution. Two examples to support this:
The Villa Lante in Bagnaia (illustration) near Rome and also near Caprarola, where Vignola's palace for Cardinal Farnese is to be found. The Villa Bagnaia was built by Cardinal Gambara and planned by Vignola in about 1573. The whole complex

Die Bauherrin verlangte eine Bankfiliale im Erdgeschoss und frei unterteilbare Büroflächen in den Obergeschossen. Zudem mussten ebenerdig vermietbare Läden angeordnet werden. Städtebaulich sollte der angrenzende Zentrumsplatz eine klarere Identität erhalten. Grossteils als Parkplatz genutzt, breitete sich der öffentliche Raum dort zusammenhangslos aus.

Das Projekt schafft hier Klarheit, indem es das Programm in zwei Baukörper aufgliedert: in ein dreigeschossiges Bankgebäude, das die Strasse vom Park trennt und damit den Zentrumsplatz räumlich definiert, und in einen eingeschossigen Ladenpavillon mit Café, der gleichsam in diesem Raum sitzt.

In einer Verklammerung verbinden sich die beiden Gebäude: Während sie sich nach aussen glatt und präzise präsentieren, hängen sie im Inneren über ein freieres Stützensystem zusammen. Entsprechend verfügen also beide jeweils über zwei «schwere» und zwei «leichte» Fassaden: einerseits Mauerscheiben in weissem Kunststein, andererseits Verkleidungen in emailliertem Glas.

The client wanted a branch of the bank on the ground floor and flexible office spaces on the upper floors. Additionally there were to be shops for rent at ground level. The adjacent central square was to achieve a clear urban identity. It had been largely used for parking, and left the impression of an incoherent public space.

The project creates clarity here by splitting the programme into two buildings: a three-storey building for the bank, dividing the street from the park, thus defining the central square in spatial terms, and a single-storey shop pavilion with café, which simply sits in the space.

The two buildings are linked by a common feature: they look sleek and precise from the outside, but they are linked internally by a freer support system. Thus both have two "heavy" and two "light" façades: on the one hand sheet walls in white artificial stone, on the other enamelled glass cladding. As you walk round the buildings the two façade types overlap in constantly changing proportions. It is as though they are married to each other.

A   B
B   A

oder

A   B
A   B
B   A
B   A

**«Die Kunst ist lang
und kurz ist unser Leben.»**

(Johann W. v. Goethe, Faust, 1. Teil, Vers 558f)

Situation 1:4500
Site plan 1:4500
Architektonisches Konzept
Architectural concept
Die Verklammerung von Gegensatzpaaren wird in der Literatur oft verwendet, um Antithesen darzustellen. Sie bietet keine endgültige Lösung, sondern schafft vielmehr ein Feld von Möglichkeiten, in dem der Betrachter sich frei bewegen kann.
Contrasting pairs are often united in literature to present antitheses. This does not provide a definite solution, but creates a range of possibilities in which the viewer can move freely.

Palast für den Kardinal Farnese steht. Die Villa Bagnaia wurde erbaut vom Kardinal Gambara und von Vignola um das Jahr 1573 geplant. Hier ist die gesamte Anlage um die Führung eines Wasserlaufes herum entwickelt. Als Besonderheit gilt der «Tisch der Kardinäle», ein ca. 15 m langer Steintisch, durch den der Wasserlauf der Anlage führt. Das Wasser wird in einem Kanal in der Mitte des Tisches, etwas über der Fläche der eigentlichen Tafel, geführt. Er dient dazu, sowohl den Nahrungsmitteln (hauptsächlich dem Wein), aber auch den Gästen der Tafel Kühlung zu bringen, durch seine sanften Geräusche weitere Abwechslung und sicherlich auch reichlich Gesprächsstoff zu bieten.

Als zweites Beispiel das Château de Maulnes im Burgund (Abbildung), nach 1556 für den Grafen de Crussol als Jagdschloss erstellt (der Name des Architekten ist nicht mehr bekannt). Dieses Schloss verbindet die fünf Sinne exemplarisch. Der fünfeckige Bau ist um eine Zentraltreppe angeordnet. Zuunterst im Treppenauge ist ein Brunnen gefasst, der ein Nymphäum versorgt. Die Dachterrasse wird über fünf Tropfnasen durch das Treppenauge entwässert. Die Gerüche der Küche im Kellergeschoss entweichen teilweise ins Treppenhaus, um das herum fünf Kamine geführt werden, welche auf der Dachterrasse in Form von Pyramiden zelebriert werden. Wenn das Sehen und das Fühlen ohnehin als die tragenden Merkmale der Architektur präsent sind, so werden sie hier mit dem Hören (das Plätschern und das Tropfen des Wassers, die Schallreflexionen im runden Treppenauge) und dem Riechen und Schmecken dank der Führung der Küchendüfte und der Rauchführung in

Palast für den Kardinal Farnese is developed around a waterway. A special feature is the "cardinals' table", a stone table about 15 metres long through which the waterway passes. The water flows through a channel in the middle of the table, a little higher than its main surface. It serves to cool the food and drink (mainly the wine) but also the guests at the table, and its gentle noise brings further variety, and is certainly also rich source of conversation.

A second example is the Château de Maulnes in Burgundy, built after 1556 for Count de Crussol as a hunting lodge (the architect's name is no longer known). This castle combines the five senses in an exemplary fashion. The pentagonal building is arranged around a central staircase (illustration). At the lowest point of the stairwell is a fountain that supplies nymphaeum. The roof terrace is drained through the well of the staircase by five drip noses. Some of the smells from the kitchen in the basement escape into the stairwell, around which five chimneys lead, which are celebrated on the roof terrace in the form of pyramids. If seeing and feeling are anyway present as key architectural features, they are here combined with hearing (the splashing and dripping of water, the sound reflected in the round stairwell) and with smell and taste, thanks to the way in which the kitchen smells circulate, and the movement of smoke in the chimneys.[1]

It is no coincidence that the two examples date from the Baroque period, a time when the senses were handled much more consciously and less inhibitedly.

The frequently expressed an

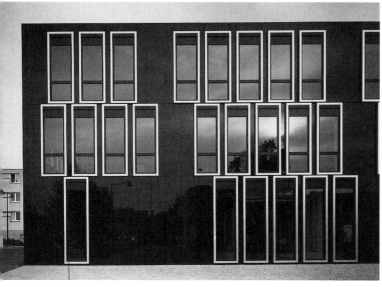

Geht man um die Bauten herum, überlagern sich die beiden Fassadentypen in ständig wechselnden Proportionen. Die beiden sind wie miteinander verheiratet.

Um die dialektische Gegenüberstellung der beiden Fassadentypen zu betonen, wurden sie am Stück gedacht und erst dann um die Ecke «gefaltet». Für die «weichere» Glasfassade wurde dabei der regelmässige Trennwandraster des Bankgebäudes spielerisch thematisiert: Jedes Geschoss teilt sich durch eine andere Anzahl von Trennwandanschlüssen. Dies hat zur Folge, dass an der Ecke, wo die Glasfassade an die Steinfassade anschliesst, die Fenster übereinanderliegen, sich dann jedoch aufgrund der leicht unterschiedlichen Elementmasse gegeneinander verschieben, um am anderen Ende, dort, wo sie der Steinwand begegnen, wieder übereinzustimmen. Ähnlich einem Jazzstück, das in Harmonie beginnt, dann immer chaotischer wird, um auf einen Schlag wieder im Gleichklang zu enden.

In order to emphasize the dialectical juxtaposition of the two façade types they were conceived as all of a piece and then "folded" round the corner. For the "softer" glass façade the regular dividing wall grid of the bank building was taken as a playful subject: each floor is divided by a different number of dividing wall conclusions. The result is that on the corner where the glass façade meets the stone façade the windows are one above the other, but they are then staggered away from each other because of the different element sizes, but then agree again at the other end, where they meet the stone wall. It is rather like a piece of jazz that starts harmoniously, then becomes more and more chaotic, then suddenly ends in harmony again.

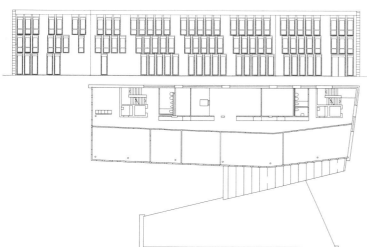

Nord-Westfassade
North-west elevation
Grundriss 1. Obergeschoss 1:650
1st floor ground plan 1:650

den Kaminen vereint.[1]

Es ist kein Zufall, dass beide Beispiele aus der Barockzeit stammen, einer Zeit, welche viel bewusster und unbelasteter den Umgang mit den Sinnen pflegte. Das häufig geäusserte und auch berechtigte Anliegen, das Konzept einer Anlage vom grossen Massstab zum kleinen durchgängig zu entwickeln, ist nichts anderes als das Bedürfnis nach Durchgängigkeit der Empfindungen. Einzelne Sinne werden eben vom grösseren Massstab eher angesprochen, andere erst im kleineren Massstab. Ein Bruch in der Durchgängigkeit des Massstabes schafft einen Empfindungsverlust.

Ein Stadtviertel, bei dessen Konzeption auch die Fassadenerwärmung bei Sonnenaufgang im Winter, der Schattenwurf und die Windverhältnisse im Sommer bedacht sind, ist ist lebenswerter. Räume, deren Schall- und Lichtführung gleichermassen vorgedacht werden, ebenso. Die «Nahsinne» wie Geruch, Gefühl und Geschmack wirken nicht allein durch Oberflächen oder Materialienwahl, sie sind auch im Massstab der Stadtplanung wirksam und wollen eingebunden sein.

also justified approach of deve oping the concept of a buildin consistently from a large scal to a small one is nothing othe than the need for consistency o sensations. Certain senses ten to be addressed to a greater ex tent by a larger scale, and other by a smaller scale. A break in th consistency of scale leads to loss of sensation.

If an urban district is conceive with an eye to façades warmin when the sun rises in winte and by shadows cast and win conditions in summer, it will b better to live in. Rooms whos sound and lighting are though out in advance to equal extent will also be more pleasant. Th "close senses" like smell, feelin and taste do not make an effec only through surfaces or th choice of materials, they are a so effective on the scale of tow planning and should be involv ed.

1 Dieses Schloss wird ausführlich von Jan Pieper in Daidalos, Nr. 41/1991, beschrieben.

1 This castle is described in detail by Jan Pieper in Daidalos, no. 41/1991.

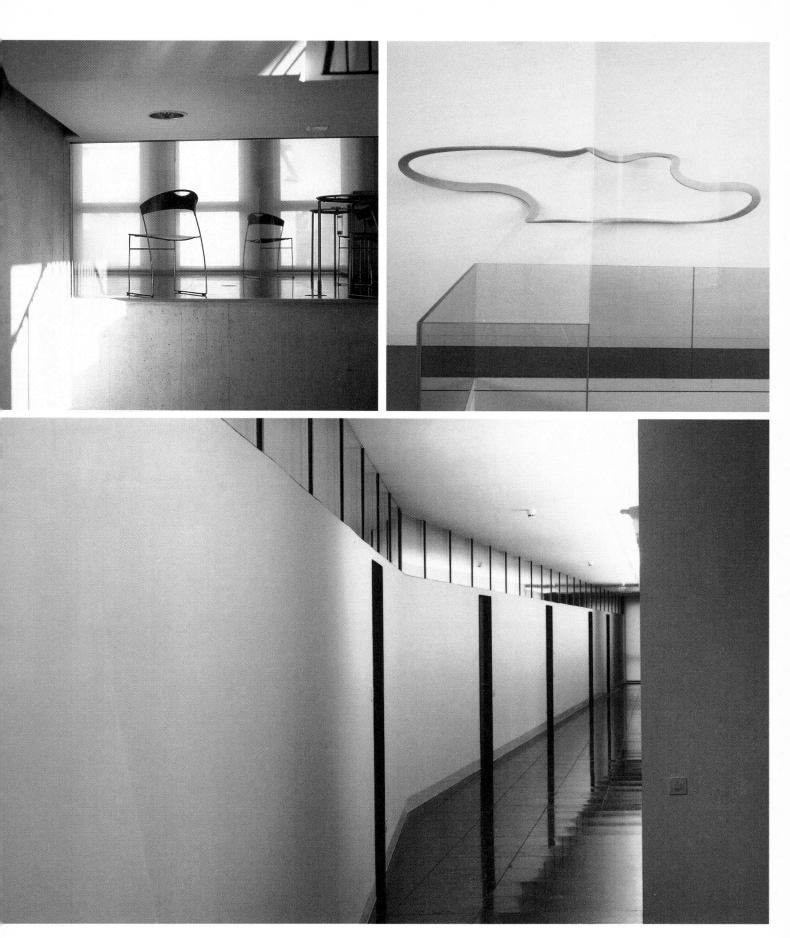

Einkaufszentrum mit Hotel und Wohnungen, Muttenz, Coop Basel Liestal Fricktal, 1993-1998
Shopping Centre Hotel and Apartments, Muttenz, Coop Basel Liestal Fricktal, 1993-1998

Die Gesamtanlage bildet den «zeitgenössischen» Gegenpol zum Gemeindezentrum bei der Wehrkirche am entgegengesetzten Ende der Hauptstrasse in Muttenz. Das Projekt reagiert auf die städtebauliche Situation mit zwei Hochbauten: einem fünfgeschossigen Hotel mit Restaurant an der Kantonsstrasse im Norden und einem dreigeschossigen Wohngebäude entlang der Quartierstrasse im Süden. Der grosse, zwischen ihnen liegende Flachbau des Coop-Centers wird dadurch an seinen Rändern in die dörfliche Umgebung eingebunden. Organisatorisches Kernstück des Projektes ist ein grosszügiger Hof, um den sich alle öffentlichen Funktionen gruppieren: Dieser Hof schliesst an die Hauptgeschäftsstrasse des Dorfes an und bildet den Zugang zum ganzen Gebäudekomplex.

The complex forms a "contemporary" counterpoint to the community centre by the fortified church at the other end of the Muttenz Hauptstrasse. The project responds to the urban situation with two high-rise buildings: a five-storey hotel with restaurant in Kantonstrasse and a three-storey residential building along Quartierstrasse in the south. The large, flat Coop Centre building between them is thus tied into the village surroundings by its peripheries.

The organizational heart of the project is a generous courtyard with all the public functions grouped around it: this courtyard links up with the village's main shopping street and provides access to the whole building complex.

In terms of volume the project consists of a surrounding plinth

Hauptstrasse von Muttenz 1:3300
Main street of Muttenz 1:3300

WYSIWYG – «What You See Is What You Get» oder: Die Benutzeroberfläche der Architektur

WYSIWYG – "What You See Is What You Get" or: The User Interface of Architecture

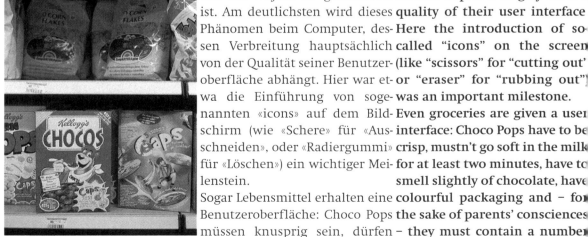

Ein verwitterter Gartenzaun soll neu gestrichen werden. In der Regel bleibt nur zu entscheiden, in welcher Farbe und mit welchem Muster. Ein anderer Ansatz bestünde darin, dass man nur die beschädigten Latten neu streicht. Der Besitzer würde jedes Jahr nur zwei oder drei Latten erneuern, und Passanten hätten im Lauf der Jahre teil an dem wechselnden Bild der Erneuerung. Im ersten Fall geht es um ein Bild an der Oberfläche des Zaunes, im anderen Fall um die Darstellung eines Wesenszuges des Objektes selber. Hier hat der Betrachter die Möglichkeit, anhand des optischen Eindruckes zu «verstehen». Der gleiche Zusammenhang von Sehen und Begreifen besteht zum Beispiel, wenn ein Kind nur anhand von der Farbe eine süsse von einer sauren Erdbeere unterscheidet.

Durch die Entwicklung von komplexen Industrieprodukten ist es immer notwendiger geworden, sich bewusst mit der Schnittstelle von Sehen und Verstehen auseinanderzusetzen. Man hat dafür den Begriff der Benutzeroberfläche eingeführt. Während einfache Objekte wie Zange, Hammer oder Schere noch selbsterklärend sind, brauchen ein Auto oder ein Haartrockner eine Benutzeroberfläche, die dem Benutzer erklärt, wie das Objekt zu gebrauchen ist. Am deutlichsten wird dieses Phänomen beim Computer, dessen Verbreitung hauptsächlich von der Qualität seiner Benutzeroberfläche abhängt. Hier war etwa die Einführung von sogenannten «icons» auf dem Bildschirm (wie «Schere» für «Ausschneiden», oder «Radiergummi» für «Löschen») ein wichtiger Meilenstein.

Sogar Lebensmittel erhalten eine Benutzeroberfläche: Choco Pops müssen knusprig sein, dürfen

A weather-beaten garden fence needs to be painted. As a rule all that needs to be decided is the colour and the pattern. Another approach would be to paint only the damaged slats. The owner would refurbish just one or two slats per year, and passers-by would share the changing pattern as the years passed. In the first case we are dealing with an image on the surface of the fence, in the second we are presenting a feature of the object itself. Here the viewer has a chance to "understand" in terms of a visual impression. There is the same link between seeing and understanding when a child distinguishes between a sweet and a sour strawberry only by their colouring.

The development of complex industrial products increasingly compels us to make a conscious effort to address the intersection point between seeing and understanding. The concept of the user interface has been introduced to this end. While simple objects like pliers, hammers or scissors are self-explanatory, a car or a hair-dryer needs a user interface to explain how the object should be used. This phenomenon can be seen most clearly in computers whose success depends largely on the quality of their user interface. Here the introduction of so-called "icons" on the screen (like "scissors" for "cutting out" or "eraser" for "rubbing out") was an important milestone.

Even groceries are given a user interface: Choco Pops have to be crisp, mustn't go soft in the milk for at least two minutes, have to smell slightly of chocolate, have colourful packaging and – for the sake of parents' consciences – they must contain a number

Volumetrisch besteht das Projekt aus einem umlaufenden Sockel, auf den zwei Baukörper wie «Rucksäcke» aufgesetzt sind. Der Sockel ist mit Glas verkleidet, das auch an den undurchsichtigen Stellen dunkelgrau emailliert ist, damit es den Effekt von normalem Fensterglas beibehält. Im Gegensatz zum transparenten Sockel sind die aufgesetzten Baukörper in aussen mattiertem, weissem Glas verkleidet. Durch diese äussere, matte Haut schimmern offene Räume oder geschlossene Volumen hindurch. Der Sonnenschutz besteht aus horizontal verschiebbaren Faltläden in Aluminium. Hier faltet sich die Haut des Gebäudes gleichsam auf. Die heterogene Nutzungsvielfalt der Gebäude hätte eine Unterordnung unter eine strenge, einheitliche Fassadenkomposition kaum erlaubt. In ihrer modularen Anwendung von Mattglas oder Faltladen folgen die Fassaden deshalb einem Code und nicht einer Komposition.

with two buildings placed on it like "rucksacks". The plinth is clad in glass, which is enamelled dark grey in the opaque areas as well, so that it retains the effect of normal window glass. In contrast with the transparent base the buildings on top of it are clad in white glass that is matt on the outside. Open spaces or closed volumes shimmer through the external matt skin. Protection against the sun is by folding aluminium shutters that can be adjusted horizontally. Here the building's skin effectively opens up. The heterogeneous multiple use of the building would scarcely have permitted subordination to an austere, uniform façade composition. Thus the façades follow a code and not a composition in their modular use of matt glass or folding shutters.

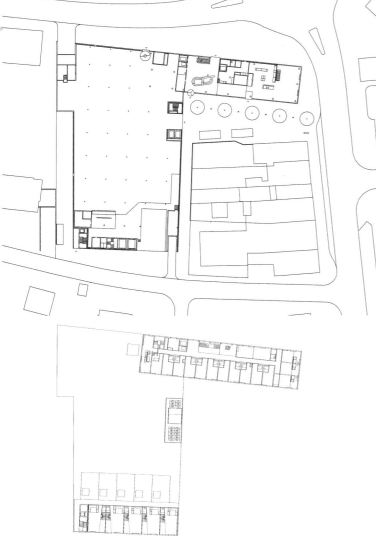

Arbeitsmodell mit Fassadenschleier
Façade model with "veil"
Arbeitsmodell ohne Fassadenschleier
Model without "veil"
Grundriss Erdgeschoss 1:1350
Ground floor plan 1:1350
Grundriss 1. Obergeschoss 1:1350
1st floor plan 1:1350

erst nach zwei Minuten in der Milch weich werden, müssen süss schmecken, leicht nach Schokolade riechen, eine bunte Verpackung haben und – für das Gewissen der Eltern – viele lebenswichtige Vitamine enthalten. Das Ergebnis ist ein synthetisches Produkt, das mit brauner Farbe auf schokoähnliches Aussehen getrimmt wird.

Eine ähnliche Komprimierung von Eigenschaften findet bei Baumaterialien statt: Dämmstoffe, Folien, Verkleidungen werden auf verschiedenste Anforderungen hin optimiert und industriell gefertigt. Am Bau kombiniert, stellen diese Stoffe kaum sich selbst, sondern meistens das Bild eines Materials dar. So besteht etwa eine massiv wirkende Natursteinfassade aus zwei Zentimeter starken Natursteinplatten, mit Chromstahlankern vorgehängt vor Mineralwolle, diese wiederum aufgeklebt auf Beton. Wie den Choco Pops sieht man auch einem Gebäude nicht mehr an, woraus es gemacht ist. Authentizität oder Materialgerechtigkeit, zentrale Begriffe in der Architekturdiskussion der Moderne, beschwören nur noch einen vergangenen Mythos. Die Oberfläche hat sich – wahrscheinlich unwiderruflich – vom Objekt abgelöst.

In der Computerforschung hat man schon seit einiger Zeit festgestellt, dass trotz der technisch bedingten Unabhängigkeit von Oberfläche und Inhalt der Zusammenhang zwischen beiden die Orientierung für Menschen stark vereinfacht. Diese Erkenntnis wird mit dem Begriff WYSIWYG – «What you see is what you get» – bezeichnet. Gemeint ist die einfache Tatsache, dass man den Brief so auf dem Bildschirm sieht, wie er aus dem Drucker kommt. Dieser selbstverständlich scheinende Zusammenhang muss im

of essential vitamins. The resul[t] is a synthetic product coloured brown to look like chocolate. Similarly compressed qualitie[s] are found in building mate rials: insulating materials, foil[s] and cladding are optimized an[d] mass produced to meet a whol[e] range of demands. When the[y] are put together in a buildin[g] these materials scarcely repre sent themselves, but an imag[e] of a material. Take a solid-look ing façade in natural stone which is actually made up o[f] slabs of natural stone two centi metres thick suspended on chro mium steel anchors in front o[f] mineral wool, which is itsel[f] stuck on concrete. Like th[e] Choco Pops, it is no longer pos sible to tell what a building i[s] made of by looking at it. Au thenticity or faithfulness to ma terials, central concepts in th[e] architectural discourse of Mo dernism, merely invoke a myt[h] of the past. The surface ha[s] been detached from the objec[t] – probably for ever.

In computer research it has bee[n] clear for some time that despit[e] the technically required inde pendence of interface and con tent, links between the tw[o] make it very much simpler fo[r] people to find their way around[.] This insight is defined in th[e] concept WYSIWYG – "What yo[u] see is what you get". This refer[s] to the simple fact that you see [a] letter on the screen in precisel[y] the form in which it will com[e] out of the printer. This appa rently self-evident link costs [a] great deal to establish technic ally in the case of the compute[r] as the picture on the scree[n] follows quite different princi ples from the plotter print-ou[t] The analogy of appearance an[d] reality is created artificially a[s] an orientation aid.

6088 31.03. 5 02362

31·12·M ⇄ E 3875

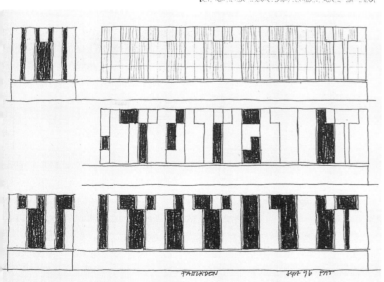

Codierung auf Fahrkarten der Deutschen
Bundesbahn
Codes on German rail tickets
Skizze zum Fassadenkonzept
Façade concept sketch
Prototyp eines Fensterladens
Prototype of folding shutters

91

Falle des Computers technisch aufwendig hergestellt werden, denn das Bild am Bildschirm folgt technisch ganz anderen Prinzipien als der Ausdruck am Plotter. Die Analogie von Anschauung und Realität wird als Orientierungshilfe künstlich erzeugt. Auch die Arbeit des Architekten beruht auf der Umsetzung von immateriellen Vorgaben – etwa dem Raumprogramm, der Zonenordnung oder dem Budget – in physisch vorhandenen, gebauten Raum. Der Architekt ist gleichsam der Seismograph, der die vorhandenen Wünsche, Träume und treibenden Kräfte aufzeichnet. Allein das Prinzip «What you see is what you get» kann ihm jedoch nicht weiterhelfen, denn seine Aufgabe ist komplexer: Er kann beispielsweise die Zonenordnung nicht einfach wörtlich umsetzen, sondern bedient sich zusätzlicher Hilfsmittel, um die banalen Vorgaben mit Bedeutung aufzuladen. Dabei werden gerne etablierte Bilder oder «Codes» benutzt, mit denen das zukünftige Gebäude etwa als Schiff-, Block-, Riegel- oder als Landhaus bezeichnet wird.

Die Verwendung solcher Begriffe hat den grossen Vorteil, dass sie im gleichen Kulturkreis allgemein mit den gleichen Bildern belegt sind, also auch gut kommuniziert werden können. Wenn sie dann aber «gebaut» sind, haben sie den Nachteil, dass sie eben gebaute Zitate unserer Bildwelt sind und somit die speziellen Umstände ihrer Entstehung oft nicht mehr ablesbar machen. Sie sind vielleicht schön anzuschauen, sie können aber den Betrachtern und Bewohnern nicht als Orientierungshilfe im Umgang mit den Phänomenen und den Lebensgewohnheiten ihrer Zeit dienen. WYSIWYG – das die Softwareentwickler bewusst einbau-

An architect's work is also based on transforming immaterial models – like a land-use programme, zoning or a budget into physically existing built space. Effectively the architect is a seismograph, recording existing wishes, dreams or driving forces. The principle of "What you see is what you get" alone will not get him very far as his task is more complex: for example, he cannot just implement the zoning order literally but needs additional aids to invest its banal requirements with meaning. Here he would tend to use established images or "codes", describing the future building for example, as a ship, a block, a half-timbered or a country house.

Using concepts of this kind has the great advantage that such images will mean the same thing within the same cultural circle, and so are easy to communicate. But then when they are "built", they have the disadvantage that they are nothing more than built quotations from our world of images, and do not show the special circumstances of their origin. They may be beautiful to look at, but they cannot be used by viewers and residents to handle the phenomena and customs of their time. WYSIWYG – which software developers consciously build in because it makes it easier to find one's way around – breaks apart. "What you see" is separated from "what you get".

In his book "Aesthetisches Denken" (Aesthetic Thinking), Wolfgang Welsch drew attention to the danger that the strong presence of images in modern life makes us "imageful, but windowless". He argues that excessive use of images in persona

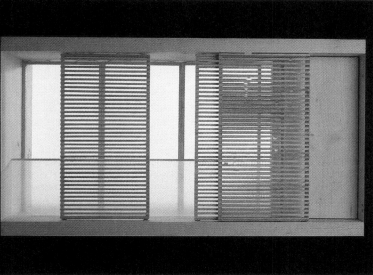

In der Autoeinstellhalle werden die Standard-
leuchten radial zum Ausgang orientiert.
**Standard lighting fixtures radiate from exit
in underground garage.**
Fensterläden im Wettbewerbsprojekt
Shutters in the competition project
Hotelzimmer «Suite», Arbeitsmodell der frei-
gestellten Sanitärzone
**Hotel room «Suite», model of the free-
standing sanitary block**
Hotelzimmer «Suite», Arbeitsmodell
Hotel room «Suite», model

en, weil es die Orientierung er- styling, consumer behaviour o
leichtert – ist unterbrochen. Das city design has the effect o
«what you see» ist abgetrennt deadening or blunting us: "It i
vom «what you get». all about being unaffecte
Wolfgang Welsch hat in seinem desensitized at a high level o
Buch «Aesthetisches Denken» auf stimulation that is almos
die Gefahr hingewiesen, dass die drug-like. Aesthetic animatio
starke Präsenz von Bildern im works as a narcotic in th
modernen Leben «bildervolle, double sense of intoxicant an
aber fensterlose Individuen» aus anaesthetic. Aestheticization
uns macht. Er argumentiert, I repeat the formula – occurs a
dass die exzessive Verwendung anaestheticiziation."[1]
von Bildern im persönlichen Sty- Take a sixteen-year-old boy fi
ling, dem Konsumverhalten oder ing on the screen an electroni
der Stadtgestaltung durch ihre gun at warriors who are storm
Unverbindlichkeit den Effekt von ing towards him. He can set th
Betäubung oder Abstumpfung degree of difficulty, i.e. the hi
hat: «Es geht um Unbetreffbar- quota, himself and thus in
keit, um Empfindungslosigkeit dulge his urge to kill with
auf drogenhaft hohem Anre- sense of success and justifica
gungsniveau. Aesthetische Ani- tion – the warriors are baddie
mation geschieht als Narkose im of course – without having t
doppelten Sinn von Berauschung take the consequences. Th
wie Betäubung. Aesthetisierung image of the dying warrio
– ich wiederhole diese Formel – loses its terror because it i
geschieht als Anaesthetisierung»[1]. detached. In architecture as wel
Man kann sich einen 16 jährigen the image of a monumenta
Jungen vor Augen halten, der am order of columns, of a ship or
Bildschirm mit einem elektroni- natural stone façade loses it
schen Gewehr auf heranstürmen- terror once we know that be
de Krieger ballert. Er kann den hind the columns is an exper
Schwierigkeitsgrad, also die Tref- sive hotel, not an authoritaria
ferquote, selbst einstellen und monarch.
seinem Tötungsdrang so mit Er- This tendency has fatal conse
folgserlebnis und Rechtfertigung quences for viewers, because i
– die Krieger sind natürlich die is only when they can draw cor
Bösen – nachgehen, ohne daraus clusions from an object abou
Konsequenzen ziehen zu müssen. its immanent powers and con
Das Bild des sterbenden Kriegers tent that they have a chance t
verliert durch seine Unverbind- understand. And it is only whe
lichkeit den Schrecken. Auch in they understand that they ca
der Architektur verliert das Bild react against things. For ex
einer monumentalen Säulenord- ample, a motorway is not "beau
nung, eines Schiffes oder einer tified" by an aesthetic image
Natursteinfassade seinen Schrek- Anyone looking at it can se
ken, wenn man weiss, dass hin- that it is there because of
ter den Säulen kein autoritärer general need for mobility. An
Monarch, sondern nur ein teures it is precisely because the rea
Hotel steckt. son for its construction is s
Für den Betrachter hat diese Ten- obvious that viewers can dis
denz fatale Folgen, denn nur cuss whether it is needed o
wenn er vom Objekt aus Rück- not. This discussion goes be
schlüsse auf seine immanenten yond aesthetic observations an

Erweiterbarer Verwaltungsbau, Sisseln,
Hoffmann-La Roche, 1994
**Extendable Office Building,
Hoffmann-La Roche, Sisseln, 1994**

Ausser seiner orthogonalen Orga-**Except for its orthogonal orga-**
nisation bietet das Firmengelän-**nization the company site in**
de in Sisseln kaum Anhaltspunkte **Sisseln offers scarcely any points**
für die Ausgestaltung seiner Wei-**of reference for designing its**
terentwicklung. Deshalb über-**further development. For this**
nimmt das Projekt zwar die Geo-**reason the project does pick up**
metrie der Anlage, bettet sich je-**the geometry of the complex,**
doch gleichzeitig durch die erdge-**but at the same time beds itself**
schossige Anordnung in die weit-**into the broad landscape of the**
läufige Landschaft des Rheintales **Rhine valley with its one-storey**
ein: Der Gebäudeteppich bildet **arrangement: the carpet of**

Kräfte und Inhalte ziehen kann, hat er die Chance zu verstehen. Und erst wenn er versteht, kann er auch dagegen reagieren. Eine Autobahn zum Beispiel ist nicht mit einem aesthetischen Bild «geschönt». Bei ihrem Anblick versteht jeder sofort, dass sie die Folge des allgemeinen Mobilitätsbedürfnisses ist. Und gerade weil der Grund für ihren Bau offensichtlich ist, kann der Betrachter darüber diskutieren, ob sie nötig ist. Diese Diskusssion geht hinter aesthetische Betrachtungen und setzt sich zwangsläufig mit dem Wertsystem unserer Gesellschaft auseinander. So betrachtet ist es eine besondere Qualität der Autobahn, dass sie nicht «schön» ist. Ihre ungeschönte Präsenz ist jedoch nicht zwangsläufig banal: Schon 1970 hat Carl André darauf hingewiesen, dass eine Strasse durchaus aesthetische Qualitäten hat, und präzisiert, dass diese Qualitäten jedoch nicht in ihrem Aussehen als Objekt liegen, sondern in dem, was man erlebt, wenn man auf ihr reist: «My idea of a sculpture is a road. That is, a road does not reveal itself at any particular point from any particular point. Roads appear and disappear. We either have to travel on them or beside them. But we don't have a single point of view for a road at all, except a moving one, moving along it.»² Seine Aussage war damals stellvertretend für eine Gruppe von Bildhauern, die das isolierte Kunstwerk verwarfen und Arbeiten machten, die sich nur über ihre Beziehung zur Umgebung definierten. Dies soll hier lediglich als Beispiel dafür dienen, dass neue technische Möglichkeiten auch neue aesthetische Werte generieren können. Man muss ihnen nicht zwangsläufig etablierte Bilder aufsetzen. Die geläufigen Vorstellungen von schön

necessarily addresses our socie[ty's] **value system. Seen in thi**[s] **way, not being "beautiful" is** [a] **particular quality of the moto**[r]**way. But its unbeautified pre**[s]**ence is not necessarily bana**[l.] **Carl André pointed out as earl**[y] **as 1970 that a road certainl**[y] **does have aesthetic qualitie**[s] **going on to add that these qua**[...]**lities are not to be found in it**[s] **appearance but in what you ex**[...]**perience when travelling alon**[g] **it:**

"My idea of a sculpture is [a] **road. That is, a road does no**[t] **reveal itself at any particula**[r] **point from any particular poin**[t.] **Roads appear and disappear. W**[e] **either have to travel on them o**[r] **beside them. But we don't hav**[e] **a single point of view for a roa**[d] **at all, except a moving one, mov**[ing] **along it."² At the time hi**[s] **statement was made on beha**[lf] **of a group of sculptors who re**[...] **jected isolated works of art an**[d] **created works that define**[d] **themselves only through thei**[r] **relationship with their su**[r]**roundings. Here this shoul**[d] **simply serve as an example o**[f] **the fact that new technical pos**[...]**sibilities can also generate ne**[w] **aesthetic values. Established va**[...]**lues do not necessarily have t**[o] **be imposed upon them. Cu**[r]**rent ideas of beauty and ugl**[i]**ness prevent us from looking a**[t] **new qualities.**

Does good architecture have t[o] **look beautiful, or at least b**[e] **academically "correct"? How u**[n]**comfortable is it allowed to b**[e] **if the reasons for its being ther**[e] **are uncomfortable?**

In our diary on "Rebuildin[g] **Höhenweg 1", Stefan Egeler an**[d] **I wrote: "February 1995: th**[e] **converted building is occupie**[d.] **New volumes are stuck into th**[e] **old one. Not to put too fin**[e] **a point on it. The façade** [is]

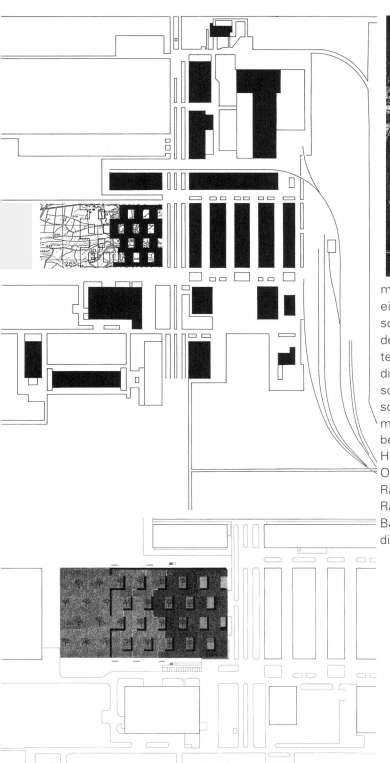

mit seinen bepflanzten Dächern **buildings with its planted roofs** eine Art «angehobene Land- **forms a kind of "raised land-** schaft» und gibt somit einen Teil **scape" and thus gives part of the** der bebauten Fläche der unbebau- **built-up area back to the unbuilt** ten Rheinebene zurück. Durch **areas of the Rhine valley. Very** die ausschliesslich horizontale Er- **different ways of working to-** schliessung können ganz ver- **gether are made possible by the** schiedene Formen der Zusam- **exclusively horizontal develop-** menarbeit entstehen. Jeder Ar- **ment. Every workplace has ac-** beitsplatz hat Zugang zu einem **cess to a courtyard.** Hof.

Obstbäume sind im orthogonalen **Fruit trees are planted in the or-** Raster der Höfe gepflanzt; dieses **thogonal grid of the courtyards;** Raster setzt sich ausserhalb der **this grid continues outside the** Bauten fort und zeichnet somit **buildings and thus is a projec-** die geplante Erweiterung vor. **tion of the planned extension.**

Situation 1:6000
Site plan 1:6000
Detailsituation 1:4000
Detail of situation 1:4000
Flugbild des Projektes innerhalb der
Industrieanlage
**Aerial photograph of the project within the
industrial complex**

und hässlich verhindern den Blick auf neue Qualitäten.

Muss gute Architektur zwangs- läufig schön aussehen, oder zu- mindest akademisch «richtig» sein? Wie unbequem darf sie sein, wenn ihre Beweggründe un- bequem sind?

In unserem Tagebuch zum «Um- bau Höhenweg 1» schrieben Ste- fan Egeler und ich: «Februar 1995: Der Umbau ist bezogen. Neue Körper stecken im flecki- gen Alten. Unverblümt. Die Fas- sade ist eher seltsam als schön. Das überrascht uns nicht, denn wir haben nie eine Fassade ge- zeichnet. Sie ist nur das Abbild unserer Idee.

Wir stellen fest, dass die Eindeu- tigkeit viele Menschen verunsi- chert. Sie fragen sich, ob wohl ein besonders schlechter Archi- tekt am Werk war. Denn – es stimmt – hier wurde keine ge- fällige Harmonie hergestellt. Je- des Ding darf sein, was es ist.»

Das prozess-orientierte Vorgehen bei dieser Arbeit ähnelt fast ei- nem wissenschaftlichen Experi- ment: In dem Bemühen, unge- ahnte Qualitäten aufzuspüren, haben die Verfasser die aestheti- sche Gesamtschau des Resultates bewusst nicht vorweggenommen. Entstanden ist die ungeschönte Konfrontation des alten Hauses mit neuen Objekten, wobei we- der das Alte noch das Neue wer- tend beurteilt wird. Einerseits sagt kaum jemand, dass er es schön findet, andererseits ver- stehen sogar kleine Kinder, dass hier ein altes Haus mit einem neuen Bad steht. Zum dritten verlieren an der Reibungsfläche der beiden «Welten» alte Bauteile ihre ursprüngliche Bedeutung. Sie werden fremd, obwohl sie vertraut sind: Ist eine Türe, die durch blaues Glas blockiert ist, eine Türe, ein Bild oder ein Schrank für eine Lampe? Die

strange rather than beautifu This does not surprise us, as w never drew a façade. It is just a image of our idea.

We have realized that this lac of ambiguity makes a lot o people uneasy. They wonde whether it is the work of a ba architect. Indeed – they ar quite right – no pleasant ha mony has been produced her Everything is allowed to be wha it is.”

The process-oriented approac to this work is almost like a sc entific experiment: in their e forts to track down unexpecte qualities the authors certainl did not anticipate the overa aesthetic impact of the resul What was produced was an ur beautified confrontation of th old building with new object with neither the old nor th new being subject to value judg ments. Almost no one finds i beautiful, but even little chilc ren can see that this is an ol house with a new bathroom Another point is that old part of the building lose their or ginal meaning at the poin of friction between the tw “worlds”. They become strang even though they are familia is a door that is blocked u with blue glass a door, a pictur or a cupboard for a lamp? Th children use it as a hidin place.

When discussing “WYSIWYG” i the context of architecture w should not refer to the classic agreement between form an function. On the contrary, “W SIWYG” identifies a central d lemma of our times. Surface an content are no longer linkec but people are aware that the need this link in order to fin their way about.

Faced with this task, the forma language of “classical Moderr

98

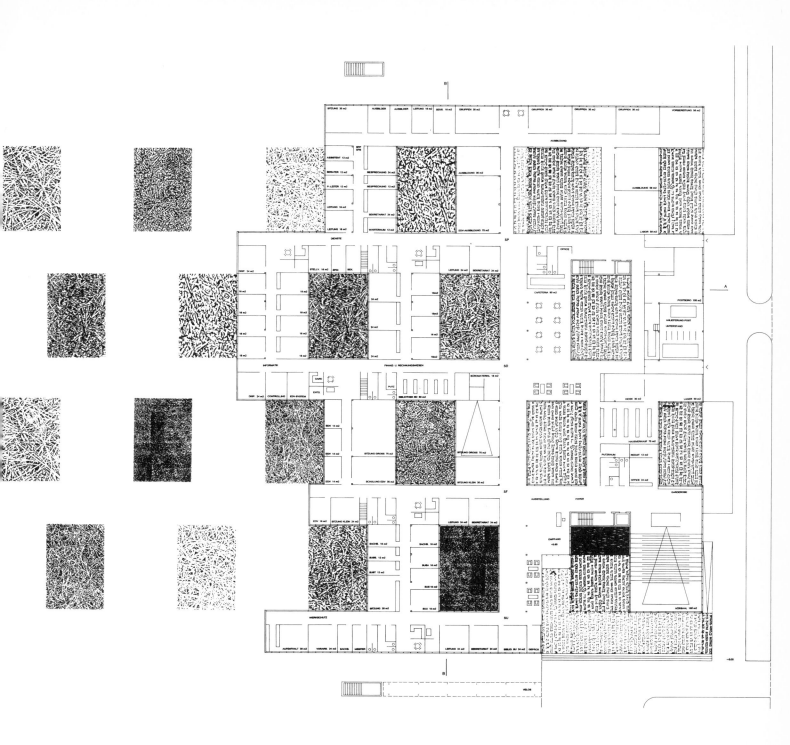

Grundriss Erdgeschoss 1:650
Ground floor plan 1:650

99

Kinder nutzen sie als Versteck. Mit der Diskussion von «WYSI-WYG» im Kontext der Architektur soll nicht auf die klassische Übereinstimmung von Form und Funktion hingewiesen werden. Im Gegenteil: «WYSIWYG» bezeichnet ein zentrales Dilemma unserer Zeit. Einerseits haben Oberfläche und Inhalt keinen Zusammenhang mehr, andererseits werden die Menschen sich bewusst, dass sie diesen Zusammenhang zu ihrer Orientierung brauchen.

Angesichts dieser Aufgabe entlarvt sich die Formensprache der «klassischen Moderne» und die zugrundeliegende Vorstellung von «funktionaler Architektur» oder von «materialgerechtem Bauen» genauso als Klischee wie die Säule aus Kunststoff oder das Eichenfurnier aus PVC. Vielleicht liegt die Lösung für dieses Dilemma in der Suche nach einem angemessenen Ausdruck für die Überlebensstrategien und Bedürfnisse des Bauherren, in einer vorbehaltlosen Suche nach dem poetischen Potential unseres heutigen Wertesystems. Schliesslich soll die Gestalt der Architektur nicht nur schön, sondern auch verbindlich sein. Vielleicht kann so wieder ein Zusammenhang hergestellt werden zwischen Anschauung und Wirklichkeit. Auch wenn dieser Zusammenhang nie wieder so einfach sein wird wie bei einer reifen, rot schimmernden Erdbeere. Schmeckt Ihnen schwarze Butter?

ism" with its underlying notion of "functional architecture" o "material-related building" turn out to be just as much a cliché as the plastic column or the PV oak veneer. Perhaps the solution to this dilemma lies in th search for appropriate express ion of the client's survival need and strategies, in an uncondi tional search for the poetic po tential of our current system o values. Ultimately architectura form should not just be beauti ful, it must be binding as wel Perhaps this is a way in which link can be re-established be tween appearance and reality Even if this link will never be a simple as a ripe strawberry glowing red. Would you like th taste of black butter?

1 Wolfgang Welsch, Aesthetisches Denken, 2. Auflage, Stuttgart 1991, S. 14.
2 «Meine Vorstellung einer Skulptur ist eine Strasse. Das heisst, die Strasse offenbart sich nicht von einem bestimmten Punkt aus an einer bestimmten Stelle. Strassen erscheinen und verschwinden. Wir fahren entweder auf ihnen oder neben ihnen. Aber es gibt nicht einen einzigen Blickpunkt für eine ganze Strasse, es sei denn, einen beweglichen, der die Strasse entlangfährt.» Aus: Phylis Tuchman, «An interview with Carl André», Artforum, Juni 1970, S. 57. Frei übersetzt von T. O. Nissen.

1 Wolfgang Welsch, Aesthetisches Denker 2nd edition, Stuttgart 1991, p. 14.
2 Phylis Tuchman, "An interview with Carl André", Artforum, June 1970, p. 57.

Baumarkt, Lausen, Coop Basel Liestal
Fricktal, 1995
**DIY Store, Lausen, Coop Basel Liestal
Fricktal, 1995**

Stuhl, du hinderst mich am Sitzen
Chair, You Prevent Me from Sitting

Installation in der Galerie Fabian Walter
Basel, im Januar/Februar 1997
Installation in the Gallery Fabian Walter
Basel, January/February 1997

Der Tisch,
der mir beim Denken hilft
der mein Kreuz kaputt macht
den ich schonen muss, weil er teuer war
der nur für vierzehn Gäste Platz hat
der so schön solide aussieht
der mich hindert, sie jetzt zu küssen
der wackelt
um den ich beim Aufräumen gehe
an dem ich mir die Zehen stosse
an dem ich esse

The table,
that helps me to think
that hurts my back
that I have to be careful with because it was expensive
that can only seat fourteen guests
that looks so nice and solid
that is stopping me from kissing her now
that wobbles
that I go round when I'm tidying up
that I stub my toes on
at which I eat

Die Objekte ███ ... ████ die Gewalt, ████ Auto ███ zwingt, zehn Stunden sitzen zu bleiben.

The objects... the violence,... car... forces me to sit for ten hours.

Falsch und richtig
Gute Manieren am Tisch sind wichtig.
Falsch ist, den Teller hoch zu beladen,
richtig, mässige Portionen aufzutun und eventuell ein zweites Mal zu nehmen.
Falsch ist, mit fettigen Lippen zu trinken,
richtig, mit der Serviette den Mund vor dem Trinken abzutupfen.
Falsch ist, trockenes Brot oder Brötchen bei Tisch zu schneiden,
richtig, beides zu brechen.
Falsch ist, mit gespreiztem Finger die Tasse anzuheben,
richtig, sie natürlich anzufassen.
Falsch ist, zu rauchen, bevor die anderen Tischgäste fertiggegessen haben,
richtig, nach dem Essen erst die Hausfrau zu fragen: Darf ich?
Falsch ist, aus lauter Verlegenheit bei ungewohnten Gerichten auf «Verdacht» zu essen,

Wrong and right
Good table manners are important.
It is wrong to pile your plate too high,
right to take moderate portion and possibly a second helping.
It is wrong to drink with greasy lips,
right to wipe your mouth with a napkin before drinking.
It is wrong to cut dry bread or rolls at the table,
right to break them.
It is wrong to lift a cup with a finger sticking out,
right to hold it naturally.
It is wrong to smoke while other guests are still eating,
right to wait until after the meal to ask the hostess if you may.
It is wrong to eat unusual dishes by "guesswork" out of sheer embarrassment,
right to ask or to wait and see how the others do it.
It is wrong to kick someone un

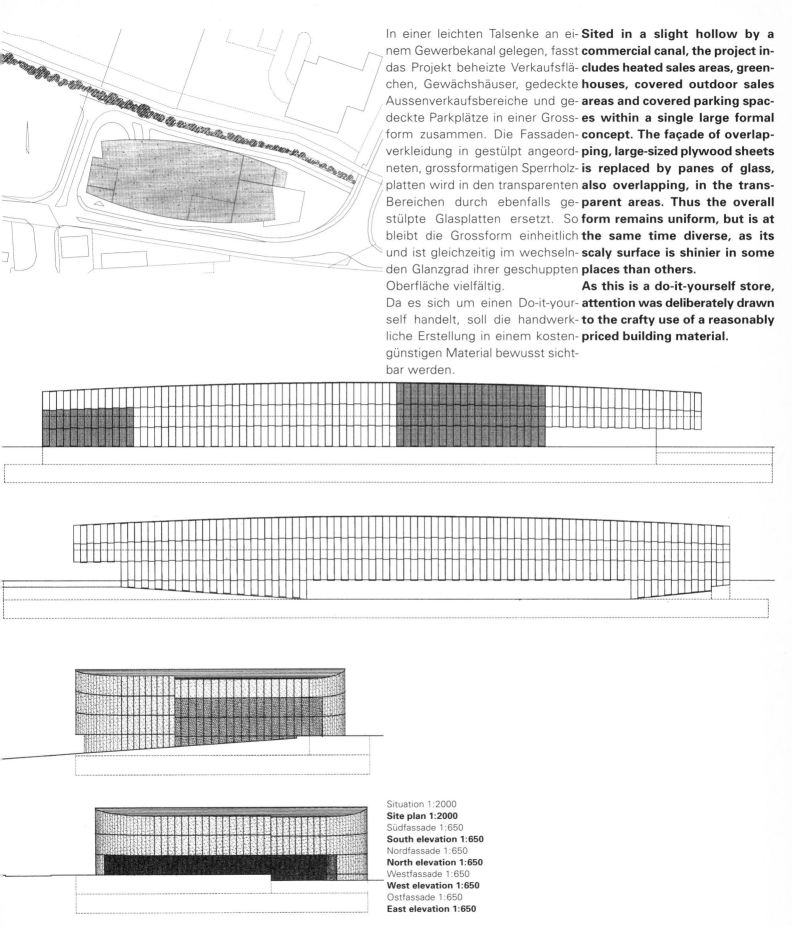

In einer leichten Talsenke an einem Gewerbekanal gelegen, fasst das Projekt beheizte Verkaufsflächen, Gewächshäuser, gedeckte Aussenverkaufsbereiche und gedeckte Parkplätze in einer Grossform zusammen. Die Fassadenverkleidung in gestülpt angeordneten, grossformatigen Sperrholzplatten wird in den transparenten Bereichen durch ebenfalls gestülpte Glasplatten ersetzt. So bleibt die Grossform einheitlich und ist gleichzeitig im wechselnden Glanzgrad ihrer geschuppten Oberfläche vielfältig.

Da es sich um einen Do-it-yourself handelt, soll die handwerkliche Erstellung in einem kostengünstigen Material bewusst sichtbar werden.

Sited in a slight hollow by a commercial canal, the project includes heated sales areas, greenhouses, covered outdoor sales areas and covered parking spaces within a single large formal concept. The façade of overlapping, large-sized plywood sheets is replaced by panes of glass, also overlapping, in the transparent areas. Thus the overall form remains uniform, but is at the same time diverse, as its scaly surface is shinier in some places than others.

As this is a do-it-yourself store, attention was deliberately drawn to the crafty use of a reasonably priced building material.

Situation 1:2000
Site plan 1:2000
Südfassade 1:650
South elevation 1:650
Nordfassade 1:650
North elevation 1:650
Westfassade 1:650
West elevation 1:650
Ostfassade 1:650
East elevation 1:650

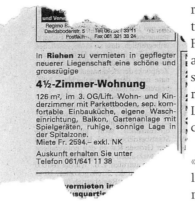

richtig, zu fragen, oder abzuwarten: wie machen es die anderen? Falsch ist, unter dem Tisch den anderen mit dem Fuss anzustossen, weil er etwas verkehrt macht, richtig, ihn leise und mit einem Lächeln aufmerksam zu machen.»[1]

«Neben den Umgangsformen spielen die Tischutensilien als Vermittler und Isolatoren zwischen den Individuen und der Aussenwelt eine grosse Rolle...
An ihnen kann aufgezeigt werden, dass im Laufe der Geschichte der Radius individueller Körperbewegung an der Tafel immer kleiner wird...
Vor einer Insel sauber arrangierten Gedeckes erfährt der Esser eine immer stärkere körperliche Einengung.»[2]

Anschauen und Tun

Die neue Polstergarnitur, der Glasleuchter, das goldene Bild: Der Wunsch nach Schönerem, Besserem ist ständig da. Die Handhabung von Licht bleibt jedoch die gleiche, denn eine Glühbirne wird so angeknipst wie der Leuchter. Aber der Leuchter sieht schöner aus, so meint man.
Viele Wünsche bei der Einrichtung zielen auf die Ästhetisierung der Objektwelt. Auf die sinnliche Erfahrung beim Anschauen, nicht beim Tun.
Was das Tun betrifft, so muss es vor allem praktisch sein. So gilt ein Sessel als praktisch, wenn er bequem und abwaschbar ist. Die Fernbedienung ist auch praktisch, weil man beim Umschalten nicht aufstehen muss. Sessel und Fernbedienung sind so praktisch, dass der Körper jeder sinnlichen Erfahrung beraubt ist. Wie zur Kompensation wird das, was man im Fernseher sieht, immer brutaler und intensiver.

der the table because he is doing something incorrectly, right to draw his attention to it quietly and with a smile."[1]

"As well as manners, utensils on a table play a major part as mediators and isolators between individuals and the outside world ...
They can show that in the course of history the radius of individual body movement at the table is consistently becoming smaller ...
An eater feels an increasing sense of physical restriction when faced with an island of carefully arranged tableware."[2]

Looking and doing

The new three-piece suite, the crystal chandelier, the golden picture:
The desire for things that are better and more beautiful is always there. But the operation of lights is always the same as a single bulb is switched on in just the same way as a chandelier. But people think that a chandelier looks more beautiful.
Many wishes involving furnishings are aimed at aestheticizing the world of objects. At sensual experience when looking, not when doing.
As far as doing is concerned it must above all be practical. Thus an armchair is considered practical if it is comfortable and washable. Remote controls are also practical because you don't have to stand up to change channels. Armchair and remote control are so practical that the body is robbed of any sensual experience. As if to compensate what one sees on television becomes ever more brutal and intense.

Ausstellungshalle Gebäude 1, Messe
Basel, 1996
Exhibition Hall Building 1, Messe
Basel, 1996

Die Aufgabe verlangt die Einord- **The brief was to place an exhibi-**
nung einer Ausstellungshalle von **tion hall of about 19,000 m² in a**
ca. 19'000 m² Grundfläche in ein **tightly-packed inner city resi-**
innerstädtisches, engmassstäbli- **dential area. The hall must have**
ches Wohnquartier. Entlang der **the largest possible stand area.**
Fassaden muss die Halle eine **The access of natural light must**
möglichst grosse, verdunkelbare **be controlled.**
Standfläche aufweisen, damit der **The ambiguity of the skin of the**
Einfall von Tageslicht kontrollier- **building – on the one hand a**
bar ist. **long, closed wall inside the build-**
Die Zweideutigkeit der Gebäude- **ing, on the other hand a trans-**

Wertung

Das Wohnzimmer ist in prominenter Lage, das Bad darf im Dunkeln sein, das Schlafzimmer ist eher privat und klein.

Wäre das Wohnzimmer sehr klein und dafür das Bad gross genug für die kreisförmige Anordnung von fünf Badewannen, davor fünf Paravents: Man sähe sich nicht. Vielleicht würde der Redezwang wegfallen. Manchmal nur plätschernde Stille.

Stünde nun ein vier mal vier Meter grosses Bett im Wohnzimmer, würde man vielleicht zwanglos herumliegen, statt steifem Sitzen mit Nackenschmerzen und Angstschweiss. Die Besucher würden vielleicht bestimmte Kleider anziehen, weil sie wissen: Bei denen muss man herumliegen, wenn man höflich sein will. Vielleicht würde die Ehe zerbrechen: zu viele Seitensprünge.

Hier wird Architektur giftig

Evaluation

The living-room is in a prominent position, the bathroom ca[n] be in the dark, the bedroo[m] tends to be private and small.

If the living-room were very small and the bathroom larg[e] enough to contain five bathtubs arranged in a circle wit[h] screens in front of them: peopl[e] would not see each other. Perhaps the compulsion to tal[k] would be removed. Sometime[s] just a splashy silence.

Now if there was a four-by-fou[r] metre bed in the living-room[,] perhaps people would lie abou[t] casually instead of sitting stiffl[y] with an aching back and sweating anxiously. Visitors woul[d] perhaps wear particular clothe[s] because they know that the[y] have to lie around in your "house" if they want to be polite. Perhaps marriages would break up[:] too many affairs.

Here architecture becomes poi[-] sonous.

Partitur

schlafen	Hocker
waschen	Tisch
anziehen	Bett
sitzen	Besen
trinken	Tasse
gehen	Tuch
sitzen	Teller
reden	Messer
essen	Gabel
denken	Schuhe
gehen	Stuhl
putzen	Bürste
kochen	Teppich
essen	Waage
schlafen	Teller

Musical score

sleeping		stoo[l]
washing		tabl[e]
getting dressed		bed
sitting		broom
drinking		cup
walking		cloth
sitting		plate
speaking		knif[e]
eating		for[k]
thinking		shoe[s]
walking		chai[r]
cleaning		brush
cooking		carpe[t]
eating		scale[s]
sleeping		plate

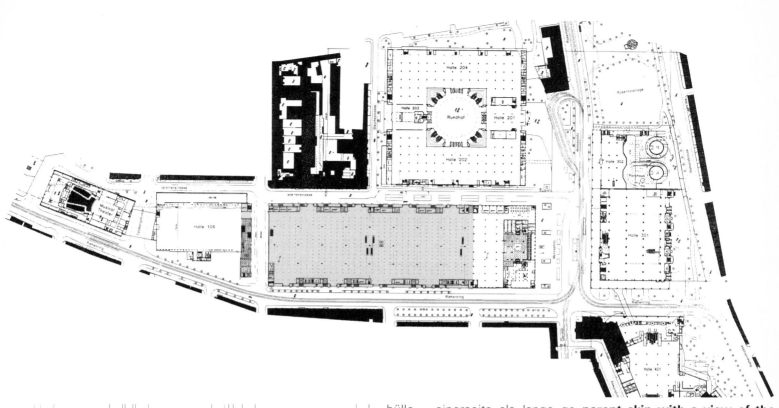

hülle – einerseits als lange geschlossene Wand nach innen, andererseits als einsehbare, transparente Haut zum umliegenden Quartier – führt zu einer zweischichtigen Fassade. Zwischen innerer Wand und einer transluziden Schicht aus Rohglas werden die Fluchttreppen und Nebenräume angeordnet. Je nach Lichtverhältnissen bilden sich die Volumina, die Leerräume und die Aktivitäten im Inneren des Gebäudes verschiedenartig an der gläsernen Haut ab. Die wechselnden Zeichnungen des Lichts vermitteln dabei zwischen Messebetrieb und Wohnquartier. Der zur Längsachse der Hallen quergestellte Eingangsbau markiert den neuen Nordeingang des Messegebäudes.

parent skin with a view of the interior for the surrounding neighbourhood – led to a twin-layered façade. The emergency stairs and auxiliary spaces are arranged between the inner wall and a translucent layer of raw glass. The volumes, cavities and activities inside the building project themselves in different ways on the glass skin according to the lighting conditions. Thus the changing images created by the light mediate between trade fairs and the residential area. The entrance building, placed transversely to the longitudinal axis of the halls, marks the new northern entrance to the complex.

Situation 1:4500
Site plan 1:4500
Städtebauliches Konzept
Urban development diagram

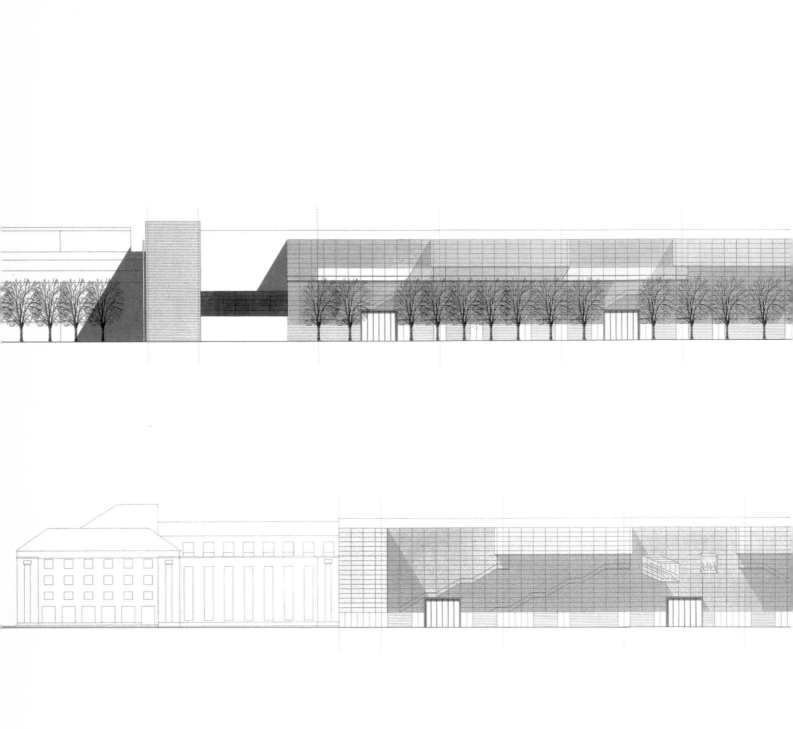

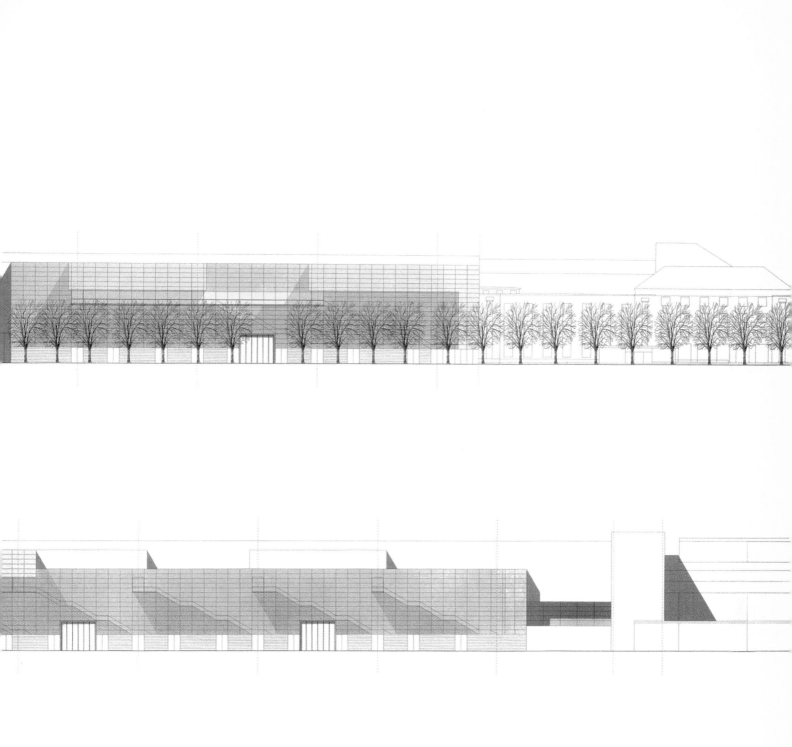

Westfassade 1:800
West elevation 1:800
Ostfassade 1:800
East elevation 1:800

Lebensqualität

Wir leben in Behausungen der
totalen Verfügbarkeit:
überallhin fahren
zu jeder Zeit
fahren
jeden anrufen
zu jeder Zeit
immer baden
wann immer man will
immer geheizt
alles essen
zu jeder Zeit
immer hell
alles fernsehen zu jeder Zeit.

Quality of life

We live in dwellings of total
availability:
travel everywhere
at any time
travel
ring everyone up
at any time
always bathe
when we want to
always warm
eat everything
at any time
always light
watch everything on television
at any time.

Als man ihn fragte, woran er sich
erinnere, erzählte er vom
Skiausflug, der im Schneesturm
endete, dass er einmal bei
Regen im Freien übernachten
musste und dass er damals
der Frau den ersten Kuss
~~██████████████████████~~
~~████████~~
auf einer kalten Eisentreppe sit-
zend, gegeben hat.

When he was asked what he
could remember he told
the story of a skiing trip that
ended in a snowstorm,
that he had once to sleep out-
doors in the rain and
that at the time he had first
given his wife a kiss
sitting on a cold flight of
iron steps.

Fernsehen

Bequeme Möbel sind
~~Fernsehen ist~~ ein Zeitdieb. ~~Es~~ hin- Sie
~~terlässt~~ assen wenige Spuren in unserer Erinnerung. Die ~~vor dem Bild~~ in ihnen
~~schirm~~ verbrachte Zeit schrumpft
in der Rückbesinnung zu einer er-
eignislosen Spanne.[3]

Television

Comfortable furniture
~~Television~~ is a thief of time. It
leaves behind few traces in our
memories. The time spent in
~~front of the screen~~ it shrinks to
an event-free span on recollec-
tion.[3]

Ich habe ~~genau~~ zehn Minuten
lang versucht, mit einer Gabel zu
löffeln.

I tried to spoon with a fork for
precisely ten minutes.

Man müsste sich einmal vorstellen, wie lange es brauchte, bis jemand auf die Idee kam, die Uhr ans Handgelenk zu machen.

One ought to try to imagine how long it took for someone to hit on the idea of wearing his watch on his wrist.

Werkzeuge

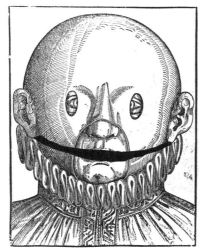

Schuhe, Mütze oder Heiztisch erweitern den Körper des Menschen. Sie sind Werkzeuge für bestimmte Tätigkeiten. Neben ihrer praktischen Funktion repräsentieren sie oft auch gesellschaftliche Werte: etwa die schwarzen Schuhe für den Kirchgang oder spezielle Gläser für Sekt an festlichen Anlässen.
Für andere Werte gibt es keine Werkzeuge: Etwa ein spezielles Glas für den schüchternen Gast oder eine Mütze für ein lebhaftes Kind beim Basler Tramfahren.

Tools

Shoes, a cap, or a heating table extend the human body. They are tools for certain activities. As well as their practical function they often also represent social values, for example black shoes for going to church or special glasses for champagne on festive occasions.
There are other values for which there are no tools, for instance a special glass for a shy guest or a cap for a lively child travelling on the tram in Basel.

«... This heating table (very popular in Japan) is an electrical device to radiate heat under the table; and if we cover this short legged table by a blanket, heat remains under the table to warm our legs.
... Oh well, I hope the spring comes soon.»[4]

"... This heating table (very popular in Japan) is an electrical device to radiate heat under the table; and if we cover this short legged table with a blanket, heat remains under the table to warm our legs.
... Oh well, I hope the spring comes soon."[4]

Sichtbar und unsichtbar
«Weiche elegante Formen bestimmen das Outfit der neuen Modelle von Volvo. Den Designern wurde völlig freie Hand gelassen. Das Konzept zieht auf sportlich dynamische Käufer. Deshalb...»[5]

Visible and invisible
"Soft elegant forms are the key to the new Volvo model's fittings. The designers were given a completely free hand. The concept is aimed at sport and dynamic purchasers. For this reason ..."[5]

Passerelle über Gleisfeld und Umbau Hauptgebäude Bahnhof SBB, Basel, 1996
Walkway over Railway Tracks and Conversion of the SBB Main Station, Basel, 1996

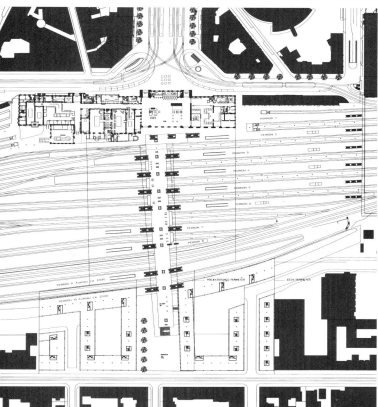

Die neue Passerelle über das Gleisfeld soll das Gundeldinger-quartier besser an die Stadt anbinden und die Bahnsteige über eine Brücke erschliessen. Dabei muss die Anordnung von kommerziell nutzbaren Flächen einen wesentlichen Beitrag zu Finanzierung leisten.

Das Projekt interpretiert die Passerelle als Teil des öffentlichen Raumes. Im Gegensatz zum Bild einer brückenförmigen Autobahnraststätte, wo Passanten durch ein lineares Einkaufszentrum geschleust werden, ist sie deshalb offen als gedeckter Aussenraum gestaltet. Ein statisches Rückgrat,

The new walkway over the railway tracks is intended to link the Gundeldingen district better with the city centre and to provide access to the platforms via a pedestrian bridge. Providing areas that can be used for commercial purposes makes a substantial contribution to the financing.

The project interprets the walkway as part of the public space. In contrast with the image of a bridge-like motorway service station, where travellers are funnelled through a linear shopping centre, it is therefore deliberately designed as a covered ex-

Flugbild bestehender Zustand
Aerial view of the railway lines (without project)
Situation 1:3750
Site plan 1:3750

«Wir haben vor einigen Jahren das Schlagwort geprägt: Design ist unsichtbar. Wir wollten darauf aufmerksam machen, dass die Zukunft wohl ein Design ist, ein Entwurf von Formen. Dass dieses Design unsichtbar sei, dieses fügten wir hinzu, um darauf aufmerksam zu machen, dass Entwurf sich auch auf den Entwurf von Organisationen bezieht: Nicht das neue Design der Strassenbahn hilft uns besser vorwärts zu kommen, sondern der bessere Fahrplan.»[6]

"Some years ago we coined the slogan: design is invisible. We wanted to draw attention to the fact that the future is probably a design, a draft of forms. We added that this design is invisible to draw attention to the fact that design can also apply to the design of organizations: we don't need a new tram design to help us move forward: better, but a better timetable."[6]

Unsichtbare Entwürfe:

• Ein Zeitschlafplan für die Bewohner. Dann passen doppelt so viele ins Schlafzimmer.
• Die Ehe der Bauherren wieder kitten. Dann reicht ein Haus.
• Die Elektrokabel in der Wand.
• Das Quietschen der Eingangstüre.
• Die Anzahl der Sommertage, an denen es im Zimmer über 32 Grad Celsius warm ist.
• Die Gesteinsformation unter dem Haus.
• Die Alkoholsucht des Obdachlosen.

Invisible designs

• A sleeping timetable for residents. Then twice as many will fit into the bedroom.
• Patch up the client's marriage again. Then one house will be enough.
• The electric cable in the wall.
• The squeaking front door.
• The number of summer days on which it is warmer than 32 degrees centigrade in the room.
• The rock formation under the house.
• The homeless person's addiction to alcohol.

Ordnung

Schnurknäuel. In drei ungefähr gleich grosse Teile geschnitten. Das Leben teilt sich schliesslich auch in sieben gleich grosse Stückchen. Sonntag ist immer ein bisschen traurig, Montag lästig, aber freitags, da bin ich fröhlich.

Order

A tangle of string. Cut into three pieces of approximately the same size. Ultimately life is also divided into seven pieces that are the same size. Sunday is always a little sad and Monday irksome, but I am happy on Friday.

Zu-Ordnung

Einem Tisch wird ein Stuhl zugeordnet, das schreiende Kind einer Mutter, ein Reifen einem Auto, ein Festessen dem Sonntag. Es wäre schon besonders, ein Festessen auf Autoreifen am Montag zu machen.
Die Arbeit des Architekten besteht grossteils aus Zuordnungen: Schlafen zum Schlafzimmer,

Assigning and tidying

A chair is assigned to a table, crying child to a mother, a tyre to a car, a festive meal to Sunday. It would be special to set out festive meal on motor tyres on a Monday.
The larger part of an architect's work consists of assigning things: sleeping to the bedroom, eating to the dining-room, W

das über die Aufzugsschächte auf den Perrons abgestützt ist, trägt das zu beiden Seiten weit auskragende Dach. Die leicht verjüngende Form der Passerelle ist Ausdruck des Massstabsgefälles vom Bahnhofgebäude zum kleinteiligen Wohnquartier «Gundeli». Zudem vermittelt die sich entwickelnde Form eher den Eindruck einer Brücke als eines Gebäudes. Zentraler Gebäudekomplex bleibt also weiterhin die alte Bahnhofshalle.

Bahnfunktionen und Kommerzflächen werden in modular aufgebauten Glascontainern versorgt. Diese bilden eine «gläserne Kette», die als Lichtträger, Informations- und Orientierungssystem dient. Endpunkt dieser Kette ist der gläserne Turm in der Schalterhalle. Er betont noch einmal die Zentrumsfunktion des alten Bahnhofsgebäudes und macht die Höhe der Halle räumlich erlebbar.

terior space. A structural backbone, supported by the lift-shafts on the platforms, carries the roof, which is cantilevered considerably on both sides. The slightly tapering shape of the walkway expresses the drop in scale from the station building to the smaller scale of the "Gundeli" residential area. At the same time the developing form seems more like a bridge than a building. The old station hall continues to be the central building complex.

Railway facilities and commercial areas are provided in modular glass containers. They form a "glass chain" that serves to carry lighting and as an information and orientation system. At the end of this chain is the glass tower in the ticket hall. This once more emphasizes the centre function of the old station building and gives a clear sense of the height of the hall.

Essen zum Esszimmer, WC zum Eingang, Bad klein, Wohnzimmer zur Sonne. Manchmal denkt man, Architekten (und Bauherren) könnten ein bisschen mehr Mut beim Spiel mit Zuordnungen haben.
Auf die Frage, ob es nun als Hexe oder als Zauberer verkleidet sei, sagte das Kind nach langem Zögern: Als Hexenzauberer.

Designkultur/Konsumkultur

Ursprünglich sollte wohl Design den Gegenständen des täglichen Gebrauchs eine schöne Form geben. Heute will es uns glauben machen, dass wir etwas neu brauchen, was wir im Grunde schon haben: Einen Stuhl kriegt man hierzulande vom Sperrmüll.
Durch seine äussere Form erhält der Gegenstand scheinbar mehr Wert, gleichzeitig diktiert er dem Konsumenten mit grösserer Autorität seine Handhabung. Man hat Hemmungen, aus einer Designerliege eine Kinderschaukel zu basteln. Durch ihren stilisierten Wert wird die Liege zum Fetisch, zum Statussymbol.
«In Konsumgesellschaften ist jede Kultur bedrohlich, die in ihrem ursprünglichen Sinn Distanz zur Wirklichkeit herstellen sollte, um den Blick auf dasjenige zu öffnen, was die Realität noch nicht einlösen kann. Der Konsumkultur fehlt diese Bedeutung völlig. Sie lebt im hier und jetzt, das sie nicht problematisiert, sondern bestätigt.
Konsum ist die Angleichung an die Waren und an deren verlogene Verherrlichung der Welt. All jene Individuen, die sich im Moment des Einkaufs frei und ungebunden fühlen, unterwerfen sich an den Warenhauskassen den Zwängen, aus denen heraus Befreiung unmöglich scheint. Verdinglichung bedeutet, dass Din-

---

to the entrance hall, bathroom small, living-room facing the sun. Sometimes people think that architects (and clients) could be a bit braver about the assignment game.
When asked whether it was dressed up as a witch or a wizard the child replied after hesitating a long time: As a witch wizard.

Design culture/consumer culture

Originally design was probably intended to make everyday objects beautiful. Today it wants to make us believe that we need something new that fundamentally we already have: in this country one can get chairs from skips.
The object apparently acquires more value from its external form, and at the same time it dictates to the consumer how it should be handled. People are inhibited about making a designer couch into a children's swing. The couch becomes a fetish, a status symbol because of its stylized value.
"In consumer societies any culture is threatening that is originally intended to create distance from reality, to open up a view of something that reality cannot yet redeem. Consumer culture completely lacks such significance. It lives in the here and now, and does not make the here and now a problem but confirms it.
Consuming brings us into line with goods and their false glorification of the world. All those individuals who feel that they are free and unconfined at the moment of purchase, subject themselves at department store checkouts to compulsions from which liberation seems impossible. Reification means that

Gemeindezentrum Reinach, 1997
Reinach Community Centre, 1997

ge den Menschen vorschreiben, **things prescribe to people how** wie sie sich zu bewegen, zu begeg- **they should move, meet and** nen und zu geben haben.»[7] **give."[7]**

Architekten und Designer wer- **Architects and designers be-** den zu Handlangern der Kon- **come lackeys of the consumer** sumgesellschaft. Wie viele neue **society. How many more new** Tassen, Stühle, Vasen, Gabeln ver- **cups, chairs, vases, and forks** trägt die Schweiz noch? **can Switzerland take?**

Ein bestimmter Verhaltenskodex **A certain code of behaviour is** wird als Realität akzeptiert. Da- **accepted as reality. In the cour-** bei werden manche Aspekte über- **se of this many aspects are ta-** höht, andere ausgeblendet. So ist **ken to excess, others left out of** an der festlich gedeckten Tafel **account. Thus at a festively laid** die untere Körperhälfte unsicht- **table the lower half of the body** bar, der Kopf ist schön herausge- **is invisible, the head has been** putzt. **titivated beautifully.**

Vielleicht könnte die Gestaltung **Perhaps the design of objects** von Objekten auch verdrängte Be- **could make repressed levels of** wusstseinsebenen wieder sicht- **consciousness visible again.** bar machen. **It would be as though one were** Es wäre so, als ob man eine **to print a slaughterhouse scene** Schlachthofszene auf ein Tisch- **on a tablecloth and then cover** tuch druckt, und damit den Tisch **the table with it.** deckt.

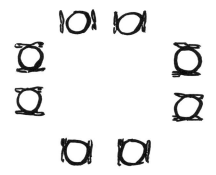

In einer Vorortsgemeinde von **A new community centre with** Basel soll eine neue Gemein- **adjacent residential and com-** deverwaltung mit angrenzender **mercial facilities was to be de-** Wohn- und Geschäftsnutzung ent- **signed for a suburban commu-** worfen werden. Städtebaulich be- **nity near Basel. In urban deve-** stand die Aufgabe hauptsächlich **lopment terms the main require-** in der Definition eines neuen Zen- **ment was to define a new centre** trums für die weitläufig zersiedel- **for the suburb, which has been** te Ortschaft. **largely spoilt by development**

Das Projekt setzt mit einem run- **sprawl.** den Gebäude für die Gemeinde- **The project uses a round local** verwaltung einen neuen Mittel- **government building to estab-** punkt. Auf Grund seiner Sonder- **lish a new centre. Because of its** stellung in der Gemeinschaft darf **special role in the community** ein öffentlicher Bau eine beson- **this public building is permitted** dere Geometrie und eine andere **to display a special geometry** Körnung als die Bauten des Um- **and a different texture from the** feldes aufweisen. Ausserdem ent- **surrounding buildings. Also, the**

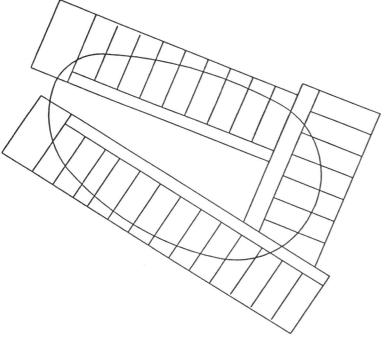

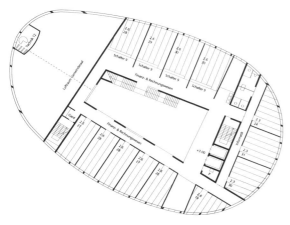

3 Büroschichten, die «abgeschliffen» wurden
3 layers of offices that were "smoothed down"
Grundriss 1. Obergeschoss 1:600
1st floor ground plan 1:600

121

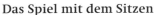

Das Spiel mit dem Sitzen

Ein Architekt muss sich Räume möbliert ausdenken. Das Ehebett mit Einstieg von zwei Seiten, Nachtkästchen und Kleiderschrank im Schlafzimmer, Esstisch mit Deckenlampe und Sideboard im Esszimmer.

Durch Möblierung wird der gebaute Raum für den Benutzer greifbar: Die Möbel besetzen den Raum persönlich, spiegeln seinen Geschmack, Ordentlichkeit, Vorlieben, Erinnerungen. Liebesleben, höflicher Besuch oder Zähneputzen: alles hat seinen bestimmten Ort. Das Verhalten im Umgang mit Möbeln ist fest kodiert: Man würde wohl kaum unter dem Esstisch schlafen.

Wenn man diesen Umgang nicht hinterfragt, wird sich das Elternschlafzimmer nie wesentlich ändern (von der Tapete mal abgesehen).

So gesehen ist die Frage nach dem Sitzen auch die Frage nach der Architektur.

The game of sitting

An architect has to devise rooms with furniture in them. A marital bed that you can get into from both sides, bedside tables and wardrobe in the bedroom, dining table with ceiling light and sideboard in the diningroom.

Furniture makes built space comprehensible to the user: furniture occupies the room personally, reflects its taste, tidiness, preferences, memories. Love life, a polite visit or cleaning one's teeth: everything has its proper place. Behaviour for dealing with furniture is strictly coded: one would hardly sleep under the dining table.

If this way of treating things is not analysed, then the parents' bedroom will never change fundamentally (except for the wallpaper).

Seen in this way, if we ask about sitting we are asking about architecture as well.

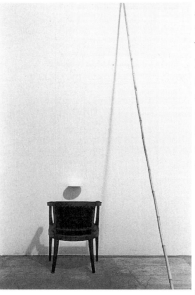

1 Renée Christian-Hildebrandt «Mein schön gedeckter Tisch» Berlin o. J.
2 «Tischsitten», in: Mässig und Gefrässig. Ausstellungskatalog, Österreichisches Museum für angewandte Kunst, Wien 1996, S. 228.
3 Otto Wöhrbach, Wie der Februar zum kürzesten Monat des Jahres wurde, Basler Zeitung, 29.2.1996, S. 5.
4 «… Dieser Heiztisch (sehr populär in Japan) ist eine elektrische Einrichtung, die unter der Tischfläche Wärme ausstrahlt. Und wenn wir diesen kurzbeinigen Tisch mit einem Tuch zudecken, bleibt die Wärme unter dem Tisch und erwärmt unsere Beine. … Ja nun, ich hoffe, der Frühling kommt bald.» Brief von Kaez Machida an Nina Klar, 1995
5 form, Zeitschrift für Gestaltung, offizielles Organ Bund deutscher Grafikdesigner, Nr. 1/1997, S. 53.
6 Lucius Burkhardt, «… in unseren Köpfen», aus: Lucius Burkhardt/Internationales Designzentrum Berlin (Hrsg.), «Design der Zukunft», Berlin 1987, S.16.
7 Peter Trübner, «Die Falle der Freiheit. Drogenkonsum als allgemeines Konsumproblem: Keine Erlösung aus der Scheinwelt.», Basler Magazin, Nr. 49, 7.12.1996, S. 6.

1 Renée Christian-Hildebrandt, "Mein schön gedeckter Tisch", Berlin, no year.
2 "Tischsitten", in: Mässig und Gefrässig, exhibition catalogue, Österreichisches Museum für angewandte Kunst, Vienna 1996, p. 228.
3 Otto Wöhrbach, Wie der Februar zum kürzesten Monat des Jahres wurde, Basler Zeitung, 29.2.1996, p. 5.
4 Letter from Kaez Machida to Nina Klar, 1995.
5 form, Zeitschrift für Gestaltung, official organ of the Federation of German Graphic Designers, no. 1/1997, p. 53.
6 Lucius Burkhardt, "… in unseren Köpfen", from: Lucius Burkhardt/Internationales Designzentrum Berlin (ed.), "Design der Zukunft", Berlin 1987, p. 16.
7 Peter Trübner, "Die Falle der Freiheit. Drogenkonsum als allgemeines Konsumproblem: Keine Erlösung aus der Scheinwelt", Basler Magazin, no. 49, 7.12.1996, p. 6.

spricht die Gleichwertigkeit der umlaufenden Fassade dem öffentlichen Charakter des Gebäudes. In der näheren Umgebung kann man sonst nur um die Dorfkirche «rundherumgehen». Die Begegnung des runden Gebäudes mit seinem orthogonalen Umfeld lässt den Weg um den Bau herum zu einem Gang durch Räume ständig wechselnder Breite und Intensität werden.

equality of the façades running round the building is appropriate to its public character. The only other building in the area that you can "walk round" is the village church. The intervening zone where the round building and its orthogonal surroundings meet creates spaces of constantly changing width and intensity on the path that winds around the building.

Vorbild für die Entwicklung des Gebäudes ist nicht der Kreis, sondern ein Kieselstein. Er widerspiegelt eine geschichtete Raumauffassung ohne Zentrum: Die Nutzflächen werden in geologische Schichten gegliedert, die Erschliessungsräume durchziehen das Gebilde wie transluzide Quarzadern. Erst nachdem die Funktionen verteilt und die Innenräume kalibriert sind, wird die äussere Form entsprechend der städtebaulichen Umgebung «abgeschliffen». Wie von selbst bilden sich die Quarzadern an der Fassade ab. Sie muss nicht speziell entworfen werden, ihr Motiv ist das Konzept.

The model for the development of the building is not a circle, but a pebble. It represents a layered perception of space without a centre: the working areas are structured in geological layers, the access areas run through the structure like translucent veins of quartz. Only after the functions have been distributed and the internal spaces calibrated, is the external form "smoothed down" appropriately to its urban surroundings. The quartz veins appear on the façade as if of their own accord. The façade did not have to be designed specially, its motif is the concept.

Biografien
Biographies

Edi Bürgin

1930	geboren in Basel	1930	born in Basel
1954	Diplom als Architekt an der Eidgenössischen Technischen Hochschule Zürich (ETHZ)	1954	Architectural Diploma at the Eidgenössische Technische Hochschule Zurich (ETHZ)
1955	Entwurfsarchitekt im Büro Hermann Baur, BSA, Basel	1955	design architect in the office of Hermann Baur, BSA, Basel
1956/57	Auslandaufenthalt im Büro Arne Ervi, Helsinki, Finnland	1956/57	work abroad in the office of Arne Ervi, Helsinki, Finland
1957/58	Angestellter Architekt im Büro Gass + Boos, SIA/BSA	1957/58	employed as an architect by the office of Gass + Boos, SIA/BSA
1958	Entwurfsarchitekt im Büro Burckhardt Architekten SIA, Basel	1958	design architect for the office of Burckhardt Architekten, SIA, Basel
1966-1981	Teilhaber des Büros Burckhardt + Partner, Basel	1966-1981	partner in the office of Burckhardt + Partner, Basel
1981	Gastdozent am Virginian Polytechnical Institute, USA	1981	visiting lecturer at the Virginian Polytechnical Institute, USA
1982	Gründung Bürgin & Nissen Architekten, BSA/SIA, Basel	1982	foundation of Bürgin & Nissen Architekten, BSA/SIA

Timothy O. Nissen

1939	geboren in Boston, USA	1939	born in Boston, USA
1945-1952	Schulen in New York	1945-1952	schooling in New York
1952	Umsiedlung nach Basel	1952	move to Basel
1962	Diplom als Architekt an der Eidgenössischen Technischen Hochschule Zürich (ETHZ)	1962	Architectural Diploma at the Eidgenössische Technische Hochschule Zurich (ETHZ)
1962	Entwurfsarchitekt bei Prof. Werner Moser, BSA, Zürich	1962	design architect with Prof. Werner Moser, BSA, Zurich
1962-1965	Entwurfsarchitekt im Büro K. Fleig, SIA, Zürich	1962-1965	design architect in the office of K. Fleig, SIA, Zurich
1964/65	Assistent/Forschungsassistent bei Karl Fleig und Prof. Bernhard Hoesli an der ETHZ	1964/65	assistant/researcher under Karl Fleig and Prof. Bernhard Hoesli at the ETHZ
1965	Entwurfsarchitekt im Büro Burckhardt Architekten, SIA, Basel	1965	design architect in the office of Burckhardt Architekten, SIA, Basel
1969-1981	Teilhaber des Büros Burckhardt + Partner, Basel	1969-1981	partner in the office of Burckhardt + Partner, Basel
1967/68	Nachdiplomstudium in Orts-, Regional- und Landesplanung, ETHZ	1967/68	post-diploma studies in local, regional and national planning, ETHZ
1982	Gründung Bürgin & Nissen Architekten, BSA/SIA, Basel	1982	foundation of Bürgin & Nissen Architekten, BSA/SIA, Basel
1984	Gastdozent am Virginia Polytechnical Institute, USA	1984	visiting lecturer at the Virginian Polytechnical Institute, USA

Daniel Wentzlaff

1962	geboren in Lindau am Bodensee	1962	born in Lindau on Lake Constance
ab 1981	Architekturstudium an der Technischen Universität in München und an der U.P.A.6 in Paris (1984/85)	from 1981	studied architecture at the Technische Universität in Munich and U.P.A.6 in Paris (1984/85)
1986/87	Hilfsassistent am Lehrstuhl Prof. Fred Angerer, TU München	1986/87	assistant to the chair of Prof. Fred Angerer, TU Munich
1987	Sonderdiplom bei Prof. F. Kurrent, TU München	1987	special diploma under Prof. F. Kurrent, TU Munich
1987/88	Freier Mitarbeiter bei Prof. F. Kurrent, München	1987/88	free-lance work for Prof. F. Kurrent, Munich
1988	Architekt bei Bürgin & Nissen Architekten, Basel	1988	architect with Bürgin & Nissen Architekten, Basel
1988/89	DAAD Stipendium an die Architectural Association School of Architecture in London (AA)	1988/89	DAAD scholarship at the Architectural Association School of Architecture in London (AA)
1989	Freier Mitarbeiter bei S. de Martino, Architekt und AA Unit Master	1989	free-lance work for S. di Martino, architect and AA Unit Master
1990	AA Diplom	1990	AA diploma
1990/91	Architekt bei Bürgin & Nissen Architekten, BSA/SIA, Basel	1990/91	architect with Bürgin & Nissen Architekten, BSA/SIA, Basel
1992	Partnerschaft mit Edi Bürgin und Timothy O. Nissen	1992	partnership with Edi Bürgin and Timothy O. Nissen

Projektverzeichnis
List of Projects

1 **Umbau und Erweiterung einer Bank-filiale am Claraplatz, Basel, Schweizerische Bankgesellschaft, UBS 1983-1987, 1991/92** (2 Etappen)

Conversion and extension of a bank branch at Claraplatz, Basel, Schweizerische Bankgesellschaft, UBS 1983-1987, 1991/92 (2 phases)

Edi Bürgin mit/with Timothy O. Nissen, Bernhard Aegerter, Eva Capolongo und/and Hans-Ueli Suter, Patrick Widmann

2 **Erweiterung der Hauptverwaltung in der City Nord, Hamburg, TCHIBO Holding AG, 1986-1989** Bauleitung Bauplan GmbH

Extension of headquarters in City Nord, Hamburg, **TCHIBO Holding AG, 1986-1989 Contract managers Bauplan GmbH**

Edi Bürgin mit/with Timothy O. Nissen, Urs Borner, Markus Küng und/and Beatrice Müller, Roderick Galantay, Stefan Egeler, Dominik Konzbul, Patrick Widmann

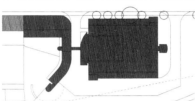

3 **Fernmeldezentrum Basel-Grosspeter, Generaldirektion PTT, Basel, 1984-1989** Bürgin & Nissen als federführendes Büro in einer Architektengemeinschaft mit Zwimpfer/Partner Architekten

Basel-Grosspeter Telecommunications Centre, PTT Headquarters, 1984-1989 **Bürgin & Nissen as office in charge in an architects' co-operative with Zwimpfer/Partner Architekten**

Timothy O. Nissen mit/with Edi Bürgin, Hans-Peter Lüttin, Claude Walliser und/and Gerd Graf, Roland Hürzeler, Donna Kolts, Manfred Kunzelmann, Tobias Nissen, Peter Steinmann, Amanda Suhr, Detlef Würkert

4 **Verwaltungsneubau am Aeschenplatz, Basel, PAX Schweizerische Lebens-versicherungsgesellschaft, 1989-1997** (Realisierung in 2 Etappen) Studienauftrag unter mehreren Architekten, 1. Rang

Office building on Aeschenplatz, Basel, PAX Schweizerische Lebensver-sicherungsgesellschaft, 1989-1997 **(Realization in 2 phases)** Study commission involving several architects, 1st place

Timothy O. Nissen mit/with Edi Bürgin, Urs Borner, Philippe Miesch, Rudolf Straub, Anita Stucki und/and Katharina Koegel, Manfred Kunzelmann, Martin Schlegel, Gabriele Schweizer, Kathrin Sommer, Jochen Timmerbeil, Andreas Tobler

5 **Lehr-, Prüf- und Beratungszentrum, Basel, Schweizerischer Verein für Schweiss-technik, 1991-1994**

Teaching, testing and consultation centre, Basel Swiss WeldingTechnology Association 1991-1994

Edi Bürgin mit/with Timothy O. Nissen, Markus Küng, Jelka Solmajr-Sacer, Marc Borer und/and Isabel Bürgin, Stefan Egeler, Dominik Konzbul, Kathrin Sommer, Patrick Widmann

6 **Dreifach-Turnhalle Gundeldinger Schul-haus, Basel Baudepartement Basel-Stadt, 1991** Wettbewerb, 1. Preis

Triple Gymnasium, Gundeldinger School, Basel **Basel-Stadt Building Department, 1991 Competition, 1st prize**

Edi Bürgin, Timothy O. Nissen, Daniel Wentzlaff mit/with Marc Zumsteg

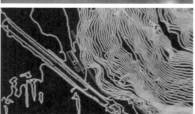

7 **Freibad «Im Schlipf», Riehen Gemeinde Riehen, 1992**

"Im Schlipf" open-air swimming-pool, Riehen municipality,1992

Edi Bürgin, Timothy O. Nissen, Daniel Wentzlaff mit/with Kathrin Sommer

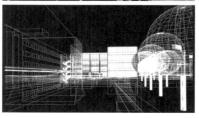

8 **Schule für Gestaltung, Quartierzentrum und Postfiliale, Basel, Baudepartement Basel-Stadt, 1993** Studienauftrag unter mehreren Archi-tekten, 1. Rang

Schule für Gestaltung (Design School), district centre and post office, Basel, **Basel-Stadt Building Department, 1993 Study commission involving several architects, 1st place**

Edi Bürgin, Timothy O. Nissen, Daniel Wentzlaff mit/with Markus Küng, Stefan Kutschke und/and Merabi Goudjedjani, Rainer Kamber, Andreas Reimann

9 **Haus Burckhardt-Vischer, Umbau und Erweiterung einer Remise, Basel, Herr und Frau Burckhardt-Vischer, 1992-1994**

Burckhardt-Vischer House, coach-house conversion and extension, Basel, Mr. and Mrs. Burckhardt-Vischer, 1992-1994

Timothy O. Nissen mit/with Edi Bürgin, Daniel Wentzlaff, Stefan Egeler, Martin Schlegel, Andreas Tobler

10 **Niederlassung Birsfelden, Basellandschaftliche Kantonalbank 1993-1996**
Studienauftrag unter mehreren Architekten, 1. Rang

Birsfelden branch, Basellandschaftliche Kantonalbank, 1993-1996
Study commission involving several architects, 1st place

Daniel Wentzlaff mit/with Edi Bürgin, Timothy O. Nissen, Marco Buner, Isabelle Rossi, Andreas Tobler, Manfred Kunzelmann

11 **Einkaufszentrum mit Hotel und Wohnungen, Muttenz, Coop Basel Liestal Fricktal, 1993-1998**
Wettbewerb, 1. Preis
Baumanagement Sulzer + Buzzi AG

Shopping centre, hotel and apartments, Muttenz, Coop Basel Liestal Fricktal, 1993-1998
Competition, 1st prize
Building management Sulzer + Buzzi AG

Daniel Wentzlaff mit/with Edi Bürgin, Timothy O. Nissen, Patricia Oeltges, Martin Schlegel und/and Markus Küng, Philippe Laplace, Hans-Peter Lüttin, Mathias Müller, Tobias Nissen

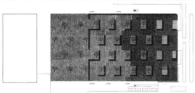

12 **Erweiterbarer Verwaltungsbau, Sisseln, Hoffmann-La Roche, 1994**

Extendable office building, Sisseln, Hoffmann-La Roche, 1994

Edi Bürgin, Timothy O. Nissen, Daniel Wentzlaff mit/with Philippe Laplace, Tobias Nissen

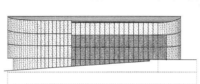

13 **Baumarkt, Lausen, Coop Basel Liestal Fricktal, 1995**

DIY store, Lausen, Coop Basel Liestal Fricktal, 1995

Daniel Wentzlaff, Patricia Oeltges

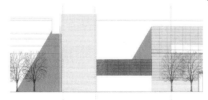

14 **Ausstellungshalle Gebäude 1, Basel, Messe Basel, 1996**

Exhibition Hall Building 1, Basel, Messe Basel, 1996

Edi Bürgin, Timothy O. Nissen, Daniel Wentzlaff mit/with Cornelia Fässler, Mathias Müller, Catherine Pauli

15 **Passerelle über Gleisfeld und Umbau Hauptgebäude Bahnhof SBB, Basel, SBB, Baudepartement Basel-Stadt, 1996**

Walkway over railway tracks and conversion of the SBB main station, Basel, SBB, Basel-Stadt Building Department, 1996

Edi Bürgin, Timothy O. Nissen, Daniel Wentzlaff mit/with Cornelia Fässler, Mathias Müller, Jean-Philippe Stähelin

16 **Gemeindezentrum Reinach Gemeinde Reinach, 1997**

Reinach Community Centre, Reinach municipality, 1997

Edi Bürgin, Timothy O. Nissen, Daniel Wentzlaff mit/with Sascha Birrer, Mathias Müller, Patrick Tilch

Bildnachweis
Illustration Credits

Translation into English:
Michael Robinson, London

A CIP catalogue record for this book is available from the Library of Congress, Washington D.C., USA

Deutsche Bibliothek –
Cataloging-in-Publication Data

Bürgin Nissen Wentzlaff:
Architekten;
zwei Seiten
[transl. into English: Michael Robinson].–
Basel; Boston; Berlin: Birkhäuser, 1998
Text dt. und engl. – Literaturangaben.
ISBN 3-7643-5806-8 (Basel...)
ISBN 0-8176-5806-8 (Boston...)

© 1998 Birkhäuser – Verlag für Architektur,
P.O.Box 133,
CH-4010 Basel, Switzerland
Printed on acid-free paper produced from chlorine-free pulp. TCF ∞
Layout and Cover design:
Meissner & Mangold, Basel
Printed in Germany
ISBN 3-7643-5806-8
ISBN 0-8176-5806-8

9 8 7 6 5 4 3 2 1

Archiv Tchibo: 11, 15o, 15u, 16-17
Association des Amis de la Maison de Verre: 54o
Bartisch, Georg: 12u (teilweise übermalt)
Bruno Balestrini: 64o, 64m
Werner Blaser: 52m
Nick Bürgin: 9u, 10, 37, 38-39, 45 ,48, 53o, 101, 103or, 125o
Bürgin Nissen Wentzlaff Archiv: 9o, 12m, 12u, 13o, 13u, 14o, 14u, 15or, 20, 21, 22, 24, 26o, 26u, 27, 31, 32o, 41, 47, 49, 51, 53u, 57u, 58-59, 55, 61o, 61u, 63, 65, 67, 69, 71mol, 71mul, 71r, 77, 79ru, 85, 86-87, 88, 89, 90, 91, 93, 96, 97l, 98u, 99, 100, 101, 103l, 103r, 105, 107, 108-109, 111, 113u, 114, 115, 116-117, 119, 121, 122, 123
Balthasar Burkhard: 100o
Corning, H.K.: 62m
Claudio Dapra/Reyner Banham/MIT Press: 52u
D. De Lonte: 78o
Deutsche Bundesbahn: 36, 91ol
Lou Dick: 81ol
Frei-Otto: 50m, 62o
Georg Gerster: 66o, 66m
Detlef Hansen: 78u
Heinrich Helfenstein: 33ol, 35
Bruno Héroux: 64u
Ann Ronan Picture Library: 66u
Hoffmann-Axthelm, D.: 56m
Humbert + Vogt: 9m
Igor Kazus: 56o
ROM Rud. Otto Meyer: 15u
Josephine Martin: 62u
P. & P. Morrison: 64u, 66
Claudio Moser: 74
M.-F. Plissart: 54u
Peter Rice: 50u
Swisscom Basel: 19
Yoshio Takase: 52o
R. Träskelin: 50o
Vermessungsamt Kanton Basel-Stadt: 113o
Andreas Voegelin: 23, 71or, 73o, m, u
Ruedi Walti: 12o, 25, 28-29, 33ml, 33ul, 33or, 33ur, 43o, 43u, 75, 79o, 81or/Skulptur: Jürg Stäuble, 81u, 82-83, 125m, 125u
G. Wagner, Roche: 95, 97or

Archiv Tchibo: 11, 15a, 15b, 16-17
Association des Amis de la Maison de Verre 54a
Bartisch, Georg: 12b (partly painted over)
Bruno Balestrini: 64a, 64m
Werner Blaser: 52m
Nick Bürgin: 9b, 10, 37, 38-39, 45 ,48, 53a, 101, 103ar, 125a
Bürgin Nissen Wentzlaff Archiv: 9a, 12m, 12b, 13a, 13b, 14a, 14b, 15ar, 20, 21, 22, 2 26a, 26b, 27, 31, 32a, 41, 47, 49, 51, 53b, 57b 58-59, 55, 61a, 61b, 63, 65, 67, 69, 71ma 71mbl, 71bl, 71r, 77, 79rb, 85, 86-87, 88, 89 90, 91, 93, 96, 97l, 98b, 99, 100, 101, 103l, 103 105, 107, 108-109, 111, 113b, 114, 115, 116-117 119, 121, 122, 123
Balthasar Burkhard: 100a
Corning, H.K.: 62m
Claudio Dapra/Reyner Banham/MIT Pres 52b
D. De Lonte: 78a
Deutsche Bundesbahn: 36, 91al
Lou Dick: 81al
Frei-Otto: 50m, 62a
Georg Gerster: 66a, 66m
Detlef Hansen: 78b
Heinrich Helfenstein: 33al, 35
Bruno Héroux: 64b
Ann Ronan Picture Library: 66b
Hoffmann-Axthelm, D.: 56m
Humbert + Vogt: 9m
Igor Kazus: 56a
ROM Rud. Otto Meyer: 15b
Josephine Martin: 62b
P. & P. Morrison: 64b, 66
Claudio Moser: 74
M.-F. Plissart: 54b
Peter Rice: 50b
Swisscom Basel: 19
Yoshio Takase: 52a
R. Träskelin: 50a
Vermessungsamt Kanton Basel-Stadt: 113a
Andreas Voegelin: 23, 71ar, 73a, m, b
Ruedi Walti: 12a, 25, 28-29, 33ml, 33bl, 33a 33br, 43a, 43b, 75, 79a, 81ar/Skulptur: Jür Stäuble, 81b, 82-83, 125m, 125b
G. Wagner, Roche: 95, 97ar

Bei allen Abbildungen haben wir uns bemüht, die Autorenrechte ausfindig zu machen und aufzuführen. Wo uns dies nicht gelungen ist, bitten wir die Autoren um Entschuldigung.

We have made every effort to identify th copyright holders of all illustrations. Wher this was not possible, we apologise to th copyright holders.